Fuel the Machine

Stand with Trump
And
See America Win Again

Be Part of Something Great

William Andrew

Made in the United States of America

Land of the Free and the Home of the Brave

Fuel the Machine: Stand with Trump

And See America Win Again

Be Part of Something Great

William Andrew

ISBN-13:978-1979339759

ISBN-10:1979339759

Library of Congress control number:2017918765

Createspace Independent publishing platform

North Charleston NC

Tweets to: Self-Evident Truths @ WillamABooks

Available as E-book

Email: info@somethinggreat.net

"We are at a critical turning point in our history, not only for you and me but for our children as well. America may be struggling, it may be crippled, but we can rise again. Our time has not passed, it is here, and the potential is amazing."

From the book: Crippled America by Donald J. Trump

I admit I am a cheerleader for Trump. Not so much because of Trump the man and what he had accomplished in the private sector, but because of what he stopped and what he stands for now today as our president.

Dead in their tracks, he stopped (big breath here) the most massive big government global establishment political manipulative progressive machine in the history of America from succeeding in their quest to continue their rule over us, and... he stymied their plans to recreate America into their image; or as they love to say, "Fundamentally" change America. But change her into what? Do they even know? Because they never explain where we end up if we follow their dreams of Bo's father whispering wind songs only the select few can hear plan. Things would get better, with hope; nothing very tangible all theory eerie smoke and mirrorie. They just needed to do more of what they were doing for another 8 years - sure...easy peasy with a shot of depresso espresso and a piece of delusion illusion on the side.

From the book: Fuel the Machine by William Andrew

This handbook is written to further unite and equip our Great Again movement. Just as importantly we invite all Americans to Stand with Trump and keep the momentum moving ahead towards a Greater America, one where the people rule again and the government obeys the people.

All by the Will and Grace of Almighty God

If you've ever thought about doing something big

Because it seemed to be the right time

And the Right thing to do

But you didn't do it, only to find out later

It was the right thing to do

And you wish you had.

Now is that time.

Have no regrets.

MAGA in 2018

In 2016, 63 million of us stood with Trump to fuel the most powerful new movement to ever jump off the starting line in the history of our Republic. We also won the U.S. House and the U.S. Senate that year.

In 2017, the President had the most successful and productive first year of any president ever. Americans are now starting to win again with lower taxes, jobs, and with much more confidence.

In 2018, the rubber really hits the road as we must push, prod, and provoke Congress to pass Trump-inspired legislation which will help all Americans, i.e. **THE WALL, KATES LAW, NO SANCTUARY CITIES** (no brainers).

At the same time the 2018 elections for the U.S. Senate and the U.S. House will happen. For us to continue to grow stronger we must elect a Great Again majority to the U.S. Senate in 2018.

America is winning again. Jump in and join us for the second exciting lap.

Be part of Something Great.

Fuel Contents

Formula Blends-Octane and Power

Preface

The shortened cinematic screenplay of "What Happened"

A young couple stood on the sidewalk after a busy day working. They were looking forward to spending some time with the family. As they waited for their ride, their thoughts drifted back to a previous time when they had more hours to spend doing things like being involved in their children's lives, going out on dates, and being active in their community. In recent years, they felt fearful; jobs were scarce and they found themselves working longer and harder than ever. Despite all their extra work it seemed like they had less to spend as prices continued to rise. They knew of many people who seemed to be doing so much better than they were doing too. What was their secret? Would things ever change for them, they wondered.

Suddenly, they were startled out of their haze by the sound of a car door opening. "Hello, are you Mr. and Mrs. Smith? I understand you called for a ride," the driver said. Coming back to reality, they told the driver who they were then sat down in the back seat. The driver slid behind the wheel and asked, "So where are we going today?"

Rather than give an address, the man, half joking said, "I'll be honest, I'm not sure. But hey, do you know of a place where we don't have to worry about all the hustle and bustle of life and can let someone else take care of our needs for a change?"

"Actually, I do. I don't have the exact address, but trust me; I can get you there quickly" he said flashing his healthy smile.

"Okay-cool, a new adventure" the woman said. "We don't need to know all the details. You seem to know what you're doing. So…yeah, let's go there and while you drive we'll just chill awhile, okay? We've been so busy we just want to kick back, do our things, watch our shows on our phones, you know, while you do your thing."

"Perfect," said the driver, "I've got this, relax. I know where I'm going and as you can see; my license is posted in front of you. I even went to a special school that taught me how to get people to this destination. I'll take care of everything. Just leave the driving to me. By the way, my name is Barack; you can just call me Bo for short."

At first the ride seemed very pleasant and the passengers paid no attention to where they were going, but it wasn't long before they noticed that despite Bo's promises, he was not a very good driver.

Bo was all over the road, hardly ever staying in his own lane; in fact, many times he was in the same lane as oncoming traffic. His speed was erratic, going very slow at a snail's pace then speeding up like a cheetah before slowing down again. It seemed as if he either couldn't make up his mind where he was going or he was just steering as something or someone else was telling him where to go. It was very weird to watch.

Despite Bo claiming he knew how to get them to this perfect destination, he skipped detours to drive on roads that were dangerous and even abandoned. While driving, the passengers watched Bo pull out an old paper map, then unfold it in front of his face and attempt to decipher directions. They couldn't help but notice the map was written in a language they couldn't understand with destinations they had never heard of.

"Aha," Bo said as he discarded the map and put the pedal to the metal, heading as fast as possible toward a big polluted dangerous-looking swampy area. By now the passengers were terrified and cried out, "Hey Bo, what is this place… where are you taking us?!!"

"This is paradise," he answered, looking back at them with his big broad smile. "Trust me; you're going to love it. Everything you need will be provided to you. But first you need a new fresh driver, my shift is over."

"No!" they shouted, "We don't like this place and besides, we are paying for this ride. Let us out."

Bo ignored them. They yanked on the door handles to try to escape but they were shocked to learn the doors were locked. Not only were they trapped, they had paid for a ride to a destination they didn't intend to go to. Horrified, they realized they had arrived at a destination they were never told about, simply because they trusted the nice smiling driver.

As they came near the edge of the swamp, the driver suddenly hit the brakes; the car came to a violent stop; grabbing the keys, Bo jumped out and ran behind the vehicle to a clean looking clearing. The passengers, still unable to exit the vehicle, had a feeling of dread come over them. They felt tricked and trapped; almost hopeless as they waited and watched, fearful of what would happen next. Then they began to do something they hadn't done for a long time, they prayed.

Their prayers were interrupted by the driver's voice. Looking behind them, they noticed Bo beckoning and calling to someone. Arising from the swamp, HRC ran towards him with eyes beaming and a smile on her face. The Smiths had seen her before but didn't know much about her.

When they came together, they embraced as she mechanically gave Bo a polite kiss on the cheek. He responded by giving her a thumbs up with a high five and a wink, all with that huge beaming smile. He pointed to the vehicle, then to the swamp ahead of it. The two of them nodded in agreement to each other. The couple could not clearly make out their exact words, but it seemed like Bo and HRC had agreed to some sort of plan when she suddenly tossed her head back and cracked up laughing. With wide eyes she looked ahead almost as if mesmerized. Completely ignoring the passenger's signals for help; she glanced at the keys dangling from Bo's bony fingers then looked again towards the quagmire ahead. She looked so confident, so carefree, so friendly, yet the Smiths couldn't get her attention and slumped down in their seats defeated and feeling hopelessly forgotten.

Bo continued talking, as she rapidly and repeatedly nodded in agreement; her frozen smile remained unchanged the entire time, still staring at the swamp ahead.

The passengers noticed when she and Bo suddenly pointed up, looking at someone rappelling down into the clearing from a huge hovering red, white and blue jet. They were unsure who this person was; but whoever he was, he must be someone of great importance. Her carefree and confident expression was gone. It suddenly changed to a sickly pale pallor and she started to wobble. Bo still had his smile, but it wasn't nearly as big as it used to be. You could tell he was deeply annoyed.

When the stranger hit the ground, it was evident by his apparel and how he carried himself, that this man was a warrior, a street fighter able to take on any foe. He wasn't the type to fight by predictable Marcus of Queensbury rules either. He quickly proceeded in stride to knock HRC aside and to tackle Bo, ripping the keys from his weak grasp in a blur of perfect speed and precision.

The passengers became ecstatic. They had no idea who this brash old warrior was, but they began to cheer for joy. They cried and laughed like they hadn't for a long time. For the first time since they could remember, they had hope that things would be better. The warrior rushed over to the vehicle and angrily ripped the doors off of it, throwing them out into the muck with such force that both HRC and Bo were splattered, completely covered with disgusting slime. Interestingly, they didn't seem to notice. It was as if slime was normal to them.

With a calm loud voice and a steel-eyed determined look, the warrior told the passengers, who just moments before were desperate hostages, to follow him to the rear of the vehicle. He told them to count to three and together push real hard and watch what happens.

Of course they did as he asked and what the trio did together turned out to be amazingly easy with the stranger's help, his gusto, and his grit. On three, with a united effort, the empty wreck glided out into the pit ahead of it and quickly sank from view."Whoa!! That was totally amazing! We're free, but how do we get back home and away from here?" asked the passengers. "This place reeks."

As they discussed their dilemma with the bold winsome warrior, they heard ear-piercing sounds coming from the swamp. They noticed fierce nasty looking creature's large and small rising angrily from the mire. Shrieking at the passengers, the creatures made threats and vowed to take them and their hero down for abandoning their ride and dumping the one who was anointed to be the next swampitician driver.

Almost instantaneously, the hovering craft that brought their hero to them landed nearby. Our warrior, with kindness and an almost naughty boyish glimmer in his eye said, **"Hop in folks. We're going someplace familiar, someplace nice. I think you're really going to like it. Believe me."**

So that, boys and girls, is what happened way back in 2016. Some thought then he was Batman. Today after 1 year in office as President of the United States, we see Trump fight everyday for our nation, a nation once high jacked by leftists and on the road to ruin. Trump now drives and We the People can Fuel this Machine and Lord willing, over the next 7 years, America will continue to Win Again for ourselves and for posterity. Come join us, Be Part of Something Great.

Chapter One

The Transformer

Directly involved, real time, in the job market as a builder developer rather than academia or government service, Donald Trump saw firsthand that the country had morphed into something she was never intended to be. Realizing it would take a citizen who had real life experience working alongside Middle Americans, and seeing no one else on the horizon capable or willing to step up, he decided to lay aside his successful life, become that person and step up.

Today, 63 million of us in fifty states are glad he did. In the true spirit of self-governance, President Trump also needs our help to Make America Great Again. From day one I was highly impressed with his common sense Great Again agenda and I realized I needed to do whatever I could do to help. This is your invitation to help our country win again by returning to the things that make America great and to Stand with Trump together as a very important part of the Great Again 63.

It's a fact America was waiting and watching for a hero who would stand with us, the average American, and work on our behalf for a change. We, of mighty Middle America, who work, raise families, pay taxes, strive and thrive, never complaining while trying to live the American dream. We who appreciate our distinct American godly heritage with its emphasis on personal liberty and responsibility, along with our extraordinary history that produced heroes who lived these ideals, not to mention the miracles that enabled this young country to become the freedom machine as well as the economic and cultural engine of the world.

For years we were silent because no one had the guts to tell us we were headed towards a cliff. However, just as Admiral

Yamamoto found out after Pearl Harbor, the American giant has been awakened and is silent no more; and frankly, we can't afford to go to sleep again.

How about you? Are you sensing this gigantic cultural shift back to distinctly familiar American ideals? Is this something you want to be a part of now? I hope you say "Yes." It's obvious the President believes in America and has worked hard his first year proving that he keeps his promises and fights for all Americans. He has great again common sense and always puts America First in everything he has done as president.

Regardless of what a person may think about Donald Trump, an honest study of how he won office shows that America truly is a country where anyone can be president. That he even won at all reveals a special call upon him as America's chosen leader at this pivotal point in our history. It was a miraculous upset win, one that could only occur in America with someone unique like Trump for such a time as this. His transformation from builder businessman to warrior politician to statesman President of the United States would make Autobot hero Optimus Prime envious and proud.

This is perhaps our only opportunity to return to greatness, to reform our government and to rebuild our country; to unite our people not around the flames of division but around the warmth of responsible and shared God-given freedom. Liberty has been the basis of America's DNA for over 240 years. It has always been a win- win situation and it will be again.

This book is intended to revive hope and action; to revive posterity thinking, i.e. big thinking - visionary thinking.

Our founding fathers thought big, designed the Constitution with us in mind, as can be seen in the preamble "to…secure the Blessings of Liberty to ourselves and our

Posterity." Posterity defined as future generations, such as our children and grandchildren, who will be either blessed or disappointed by what we did for them today and what we leave them tomorrow. Our founding fathers passed the torch of liberty to us. Are we going to let the flame go out?

America was based on freedom and self-governance. This radical concept made her rich with innovation, strong in principle, foresight, bravery, fortitude and kindness. Just as in those early days, we must once again look out for each other, as Americans were prone to do and have done for centuries. We've all been deeply blessed together whether we know it or not.

Abraham Lincoln best described the machine as ***"government of the people, by the people, for the people,"*** one that runs best when more of us thoughtfully and carefully fuel it, avoiding anything that would dilute or pollute it causing it to stall or not run as designed, jeopardizing the rights of all of us.

Do you want America to be independent and strong again for us today and posterity tomorrow? That was America by tradition but not so much in recent practice. Things were getting very shaky, weren't they? We sensed that our interests were ignored to the point that we were made weak and left vulnerable. That is, until we stepped up and put Trump in the White House.

Until Trump, not only was the machine hijacked, it was treated like a rare antique: tarped and stored out of view in a remote location. Yes, a very valuable ride but only a select few had access to. This, of course, is completely contrary to representative government since we the people own it and it was custom built for us. It was built to win for us.

Trump has made the machine far more accessible to us than it was. All we need to do and must do is fuel it.

Each of us has the freedom and power to make a difference in our country or at least, we should try to leave it in better shape than it was when given to us. We make a difference when we transform ourselves like Trump did from silent citizens into fuel to power the machine of our people-powered government. Fueled by our voices, our ideas, our directives, and poured into our representative government machine in massive quantities; causing it to once again reflect the constitutional will of "we the people."

In case you're thinking to yourself *I Can't*.

"Old Man Can't is dead. And I helped bury him"
—*Myers Anderson* Former Slave and grandfather of Clarence Thomas of the SCOTUS

A Mind Headline:

Trump Upset Victory Courtesy of Very Upset Americans

Trump to America: "You May Get Bored With Winning! But I Don't Think So"

What is the Fuel of American government? Well, it's you and I. We are the Fuel and in fact we each own part of the machine. We inherited it, we have the operation manual, we power it and just as a car will not run very long if it does not have routine and frequent maintenance; without us, the machine of government will not run very well and obviously it hasn't run well for decades.

Fuel is anything that produces energy, power and heat. Three interesting applicable ideas… Energy…Power… Heat or simply EPH. Let's look at them quickly.

We are the Fuel that gives the machine of government EPH.

The amount of EPH is dependent on how good the fuel is and how that fuel gets injected into the engine/ machine or IF it gets injected at all.

Fuel produces useful Energy when first it undergoes reaction, and that reaction produces power and power produces heat. We are the fuel source; we are the power for the machine.

As in a real engine, the reaction begins with a spark. Much like the gas grill when you turn on the fuel, hit the spark button, or throw in a match. The spark ignites the fuel and produces energy, power, and heat.

Trump was the spark that caused our reaction. **BOOM**

Energy: First we reacted to Trump as he sparked the Great Again movement. Beyond the spark idea Trump literally fracked a buried source of unknown untapped energy with an explosive charge. Our newly released energy freed us from our reliance upon low energy freedom limiting swampiticians. **BOOM**

Next-Power: Our fuel powered his presidency to win.

And now-Heat: Together we, as in you, I, and the President will fuel the Great Again agenda with our combined energy and power and heat. America is back and out on the track again. (Keep in mind that our race runs on for many years with many obstacles set up by our opponents for 2018 and 2020.)

How will the Great Again 63 do it?

Some of us will do things with money, some with ideas, some with action, writing letters to congress, and some will run for office; together we push congress to support the Great Again agenda. Still others will strive to convince the other side or the non-involved to be involved and that the Prog/Progressive way is off the cliff, not sustainable and will wreck America.

But all of us must use the power of our vote again.

Our vote is the ultimate source of our power.

Make America Think Again.

Imagine with me what our country would be like without our involvement.

If you can't imagine it, just open the home page on your Internet news site, newspaper, or view your cable channel. What we really see, if you think about it, is a reflection of a society devoid of our good ideas, our energy, our steadiness, our vision our values.

Things Stranger (The Show)

Before the involvement of our Great Again 63, America faced an unchallenged "Upside Down" that had us living in confusion and ever growing fear.

No one seemed to know how we ended up with it or what the thing really was, let alone where it came from or how we could stop it. That is until Trump (Think Sherriff Hopper here).

It's as if underneath America was a network of vast tunnels undermining almost everything going on above at the surface.

Hidden from view powerful creatures of division, confusion and darkness used the network to spread and grow stronger; taking control over parts of the country and many of our people. However, our everyday people didn't realize the danger they too were in or that they too were under some form of strange alien control even though they could see some sort of unexplainable slime on various parts of the land.

The tunnels went undetected for a long time, but a few acutely aware people, that had family and friends terribly harmed by the darkness, decided to stand up together, along with the Sherriff and break in to the source of the problem even though the darkness seemed to be vastly stronger than they.

Weak as they were as individuals they learned quickly that together they could do the impossible. And they did. They risked everything to keep and protect the people they loved from danger. With Trump so shall we.

Impossifuel

That's what I'm talking about: Doing the Impossible Together.

Trump's win was "Impossible", but we did it together.

America made Great Again "Impossible"?

Draining the Swamp "Impossible"?

America made Safe Again "Impossible"?

63 million United Americans "Impossible"?

A 63 million AND growing movement "Impossible"?

Electing a "Great Again" Congress in 2018 "Impossible"?

Re-electing Trump-Pence in 2020 "Impossible"?

Together we can do what others tell us is impossible.

Stay acutely aware of and keep reminding each other of the idea that I am, you are, and all of us together are very important to America; very important indeed. This is our time to do the impossible together.

Don't let the darkness of the "upside down" divide and weaken us again. It wants us to feel powerless-insignificant.

Motivational Mottos

"With God all things are possible" State Motto of Ohio.

"United We Stand Divided We Fall" State Motto of Kentucky.

"Under God the People Rule" State Motto of South Dakota.

"In God We Trust" State Motto of Florida.

Here is proof of how we power our government from one powerful sentence of our Declaration of Independence: **"Governments are instituted among Men, deriving their just powers from the consent of the governed."**

Our consent, yours and mine, is the fuel.

Everything the government has or does is because we either gave it permission, or we silently allowed it to do what it does; everything. But…things have changed.

The Great Again agenda is not complicated.

We will think again.

We will be really free again.

We will be safe again.

We will be rich again and generous again.

We will be strong again.

We will think generationally again.

We will ask God to bless us again.

We will be united again.

While I listed unity last, it is truly the most important aspect or fruit of a Great Again America. Unity is a reflection of God's blessing. If God doesn't bless us, there is division, and when he does bless, there is unity and tranquility.

1,8,4,3,6,5,7,2 The Order of a Smooth Running Machine

It's been imbedded in my mind since I was 15; it is the sequential cylinder firing order of my 396 Cubic Inch Chevy motor. I memorized it after I accidentally put the ignition wires on the wrong spark plugs resulting in fire shooting out of the top of the motor through the carburetor, burning some of my rather long hair off as it deafened me with a sound like that of a shot gun. Regaining composure, I studied the manual to find my mistake. I had the firing order out of sequence and the machine would never run well due to my mistake. The manual showed me the problem, I switched 2 or 3 ignition wires and voila! It started up and ran like a champ.

There will never be harmony when we ignore the manual. Each of us is important. Each of us is equal. If there is fire and noise and we can't get anywhere, something isn't right. If we've been burned, don't do the same thing over again. Never give up until it runs as it should and takes us where we want it to take us. Switching just a few wires will help the machine purr as well as return it to its designed maximum powerful performance. America First is just the tune up we needed.

Dash Light-Warning-Warning-Warning-Warning

Before we forget about him, that old driver Bo somehow became a multi-millionaire and as we speak is developing a band of swampiticians to try to convince the gullible that the swamp is still paradise. We need to watch out for Bo and warn others about his work to undermine our President and the new direction we are going in.

Bo now drives a new vehicle called Organizing for Action or OFA. Basically, he pulled his old vehicle out of the swamp to use it to train others to do what he did while he was the driver. Draw your conclusions as to the motives of the man. Donors have contributed millions of dollars, and allegedly 30,000 volunteers continue to push his agenda of "fundamental change" from a couple hundred offices throughout the USA. OFA is "dedicated to empowering progressive talent at every level". This is a serious challenge to the will of the American people and our liberty. That's another reason why I was compelled to write this book. Bo is an unprecedented political meddler. Every time he gets involved proves his great disrespect for America, our core values, Trumps victorious election and reveals Bo's love for big government global socialism. That goes double for Obama's apprentice Hillary Clinton as well.

What does that even mean "progressive talent"? Does it mean people who look good with big smiles and big degrees, with big connections and big money who give clever speeches that promise to give big things yet never reveal how they can do what they claim? Okay. Just leave a few ignition wires off, right? No way... we've been burned once, never again, Bo.

OFA is one of several progressive left organizations working against The Great Again agenda. It seeks to preserve the swamp and help establishment, centrist, leftist politicians retain their power as they grow government bureaucracy and its control over every aspect of our lives. This is all to our detriment and against everything America was ever intended to be.

The professional Prog political class had a good track record of winning reelection and remaining entrenched in Washington, but it doesn't have a very good history of winning for America.

They are proven experts at tying our hands and limiting our potential. Making complex the simple is their brand and trademark; talented in illusion and subterfuge dot conartists. We see them as the blind leading the lied to.

You will learn much more about the political left at: **discoverthenetworks.org**

While on the site, click "Politics", in the "resources" column click "The Cloward-Piven Strategy." After you look it over I think you'll agree with me that we must never allow the progressives in power again. EVER!

This site is a great one to learn what leftist financier George Soros is doing. He recently donated $18 billion dollars to his "Open Society Foundations" which support a network of 40 foundations, funding (of course) Democrat progressives, globalism, open borders, and other non-sustainable policies that would wreck America permanently. A lot of them sound good too for example: Center for American Progress, or Indivisible, or Media Matters.

A quote, to perhaps prepare ourselves to deal with these elites and their minions, from the humor and wisdom of ***Mark Twain:***

"Never argue with stupid people, they will drag you down to their level and then beat you with experience."

It's a witty reminder for us to fight with ideas and ballots, not with uninformed bozos who think socialism is innocent charity and controllable; when it is really an incentive-zapping dangerous collective of power that ends up in the hands of a select few "Central Planners" that give to some what they've taken from others. Progressive socialism is certainly not sustainable and not the legacy we want to leave our posterity, besides it has never worked successfully anywhere without taking God- given rights away from people. Hello.

Does government create wealth? No, of course not and neither does it invent or produce or plant or build or manufacture. But it does control who wins and who loses as well as what is taught and what isn't taught. So if we the people don't control government, then who does? If it isn't the people, who then controls who wins? Hint: look at the growth and multiplying prosperity around DC.

Here is how our first president defined government:

"Government is not reason, it is not eloquence, it is force; like fire, a troublesome servant and a fearful master." --*George Washington*

Keep President Washington's definition in mind. May we all, as best we can, explain and lead others to conclusions that are realistic, sustainable and reliable as we fuel the machine and stand with President Trump in the exciting days ahead.

Excitement in Serious Days

Some of the obvious dangers around us are: terror, drugs, unemployment, and racism, but they pale and are truly secondary to the huge internal problem of a **divided America**. There are many forms of division besides racial ones, but behind most division is the fear or the feeling of being cheated and misled, even harmed intentionally.

We must acknowledge that there are intentional dividers whose sole interest is to prevent divisions from healing. Again, draw your own conclusions as to their motives. Part of the remedy is to simply switch a few wires on the machine. Yeah, throw them out of office. The fire and noise will stop. We'll then be able to go somewhere instead of spinning our wheels.

There is a truth as true as the law of gravity and as simple: united we stand, divided we fall. Visualize the country transforming from a divided nation into a united one. No more fire or noises, just smooth and powerful like my old 396. Of course, it will take some work but the results will be well worth it. And... if we're going to fight... we should fight for each other.

The First Thing

The first thing is to be sure that we of the Trump 63, as in 63 million, pull close together to become and remain the most united, powerful, clear-minded, rational visionary force on this planet since the days of World War II. They faced serious threats back then and won. Americans back then were so united that the idea of disagreeing over the common goal of winning against the Axis alliance was unheard of. Freedom depended on them fending off attacks from within and without. They had to defeat the enemy or loose America forever. They had to win and so do we.

If the Nazis and the Empire of the Sun had emerged victorious, America, and indeed the world today would be in slavery to an ideology that was, without a doubt, ruthless, dictatorial, unfair, barbaric, godless, and murderous. You would never be reading this and I would never have been permitted to write about it.

My hope is that you will not just read this book, but use it for reference and motivation. I know you will find renewed inspiration for just how important, how vital, and how powerful you are, and we are; to each other and to this great country. All of us! The bottom line is this: I can't make you or anyone else act. You must act on your own and when you do you will never be the same.

United: Transformed and on a noble needed journey, Our destination: A Great America.

Together by God's grace, let's shake off complacency and resist time-wasting distractions or coasting along in the back of the car, imagining that someone else will do the right things for the nation and for our posterity. We must resist thinking that since Trump is now in office and has done extremely well his first year that all is well, roll over and head back to Silentville to our comfy home on Snoozy Street. This type of attitude has resulted in several military defeats, including our own at Pearl Harbor, and ironically Japans in the Battle of Midway, which changed the course of the Pacific War.

In recent history, America went to sleep following the first attack on the World Trade Center in 1993. At trial, it was admitted the plan was to cause the north tower to collapse and fall into the other tower, bringing them both down. Because the attack failed its objective, we became complacent, thus setting the stage for 9/11/01 where the enemy finished what they started back in 1993.

We are needed more than ever in this revival for a better future. Always keep in mind that many hands make any load much lighter. We have at least 3 and probably 7 years to have Trump in office. It will take all of them to Make America Great Again for us today and for posterity tomorrow.

Don't be conformed; be transformed by the renewing of your mind so you can do the will of God (Romans 12:2).

"What would life be if we had no courage to attempt anything?" --*Vincent Van Gogh*

"Fear Not"—*Almighty God.*   This is so cool… the phrase "Do not be afraid" or its variation, is written in the Bible 365 times. This is our daily reminder to live each day fearlessly.

We are already seeing that a Great America is a simpler America. Regulations, paperwork, red tape complications are, as you read, being and will continue to be overhauled, disassembled, and streamlined.

Why?

The new boss, our Manhattan Marshall, is a customer oriented guy. He is used to putting his customers, his residents first. With Trump we are first again. With Trump, we are ignored no more. Finally, we have a chance to help America win again; a great victory for us and our posterity. Going in a new direction feels really good.

Congress Must Comply

Later, we'll learn how to get congress to perk up. They must move our Great Again agenda down the road. Let's move the Great Again agenda into the express lane, and if Congress resists; we fire every last one of them, thus switching a few wires on our machine.

The Head and Heart Part

What can you and I do today to have the kind of powerful united mindset in our heads and hearts that the previous generation had in their heads and hearts during the WWII era? Yes, they had great leadership back then and now so do we today in President Trump. Obviously, some Americans need to stop long enough to listen to him and tune out the Prog fraudcasters who dislike him and his ideas; ideas that 63 million of us agree with.

It's simple, really; here is what we do: We look to the same things the greatest generation looked to, the same things our founders looked to. Keep a pen with you as you read through this book. When you get an idea, jot it in the book. You never know, you may think of something Congress or even the President needs to know about; don't short yourself; remember you are EPH.

Look

*To the God of Creation**. See his self-evident truths prevail, from the face of the moon to the face of a baby; from the light of the sun to the light of a candle. God made all of creation. All of it- no excuses- God made it all.

*To the word of God:** The Holy Scriptures contain Instruction and history, both law and liberty; from the Ten Commandments to the forgiving plan and grace of Jesus Christ, who rose from the dead and is returning. Call it the food or fuel for the soul of man and of nations.

*To the US Declaration of Independence**. Read it; be inspired to know that our founders fought a royal swamp similar to the entrenched swamp we fight against today. Its words are so relevant; only the names have changed. Take just a few minutes to read it. It will inspire you.

*To the US Constitution**. The manual for operating our machine today and the beauty of it is that it was written as a simple structure, built so the common man could understand it; no law degree required.

*Look to our President**. Just as in World War II, we have a President who inspires us with his "can do" skills and attitude. He is exactly what we need today. He can say "let's do" because he "did do" so many great things throughout his life.

The swamp is so afraid of our Great Again movement because they know their gravy train and usurping of our rights is coming to an end (with our efforts). They are in a panic; which can be seen by the obvious fabrications they spin out. Unlike other presidents who owed their election to those who paid for his campaign and a compliant media, President Donald Trump owes no one ANYTHING, except We the People. Now, isn't that refreshing and a welcomed major change, but a danger apparently to the establishment, hence the shrieks from the swamp. Oh well.

It seems their Russia narrative fizzled and they've created Antifa. Someone very clever has convinced gullible (OFA people?) to fight "Fascism" by using fascist thug tactics, forgetting that we are now led by a capitalist who cherishes our Constitution.

*Look to each other. From sea to shining sea, in brotherhood with fierce unity to become more and do more together than perhaps we've ever done before.

Dos and Don'ts

 * **We must hold our Congressman accountable** to support the Trump agenda, our agenda; the Great Again agenda. If they won't deliver it, we will replace them- no matter what party, and we will do so by using the primary system. There's no sense in letting the rats hold our cheese any longer.

*What we won't do is protest, scream, fight, be violent, light fires, throw bombs, threaten harm, or put ourselves in harm's way. You'll read more than a few times that we simply need to schedule time to preserve freedom. We will "walk softly and carry a big stick" of ideas to correct the deep mess that the "professional" politicians have made of things. Let others, by their actions, discredit their progressive agenda.

Let's keep our Great America agenda fresh, clear, honest and inviting.

Our Greatest Weapons

Prayer and action are needed big league for our 45th President. Encourage him by going to his rallies. Write him to show your support for him, his plans and his actions. Believe me, he appreciates our support. Praying will help him more than anything. I believe prayer was the secret weapon behind why he won office. No poll on earth can reveal, predict, or take into account the effects of prayer and God's hand in any election or in decisions or in victory. None.

Here and now, let's do some excavating and clear up something about the President, or for that matter, any man or woman on the planet. Although he is President, he is not perfect and never was. I'm certainly not, and neither are any of the president's vicious, repetitious critics whose only intentions seem to be keeping division and false controversy alive the entire time Trump is President. My question: are you perfect? Is anyone alive today perfect?

Who among us has not slipped? Who of us has not sinned? Who has never hated or lied or known jealousy, or selfish ambition, pride, or never known the craving lust of the eyes or sensual pulls of the body? Maybe even smaller issues like not being genuinely thankful for what we have, for our health or our country. *We all fall short* of perfection, that's for sure.

If someone thinks they're perfect, throw the first stone. Hold onto that stone for a while, perhaps to later build something useful with it or as a reminder of a stone once cast in haste.

The Intention

An intention throughout my book (there are several) is to unite all of us around common sense distinct American ideals and standards that were established early in America. Why? Because they work and are the only reason we've lasted this long as a Constitutional Republic.

Many millions of us are greatly inspired by the practical ideas of our President. He uncovered and now discovers problems the political establishment has ignored for many years. As more problems are uncovered, the left will scream even more in an attempt to create a distraction and divert attention from the very problems they helped create in the first place!

We know this: Together our combined efforts; his, yours and mine, will produce results far above what any of us would ever be capable of accomplishing separately on our own. That is the power and strength that comes from Unity, Great unity that is distinctly American. Synergy.

Think of it this way: you and I get to help the President drive the country to the destination that best makes sense to us rather than blindly trusting a driver. He needs our fuel to get there and we need him to drive us. That's our movement and our motive. Period.

The Results

I realize this is yesterday's news, but it's motivating for us to look back at our amazing win every now and then.

Electoral votes: Trump 304; Hillary 227.

States won: Trump 30; Hillary 20.

Counties won: Trump 2,623; Hillary 489.

With 63 million votes going to Trump, America paused on bended knee to thank God, while a tiny percentage of the defeated resorted to other things.

With the election war over, despite those who are like the island-bound Japanese soldier who didn't know he lost the war; the victor laid legitimate claim to his authority and is now putting his ideas into action, with the help and passion of the people who fought to elect him.

Previously, back when defeated politicians had class, they were called the "loyal opposition." What this meant was that although they supported the president's opponent during the election, afterwards, they provided support for most anyone elected out of respect for the people who elected them and in honor of America's amazing and constitutionally-based electoral system. The phrase we used to hear was "respect the office, even if you can't respect the man."

Our challenge now is how to implement Trump's ideas, our ideas, into effective policy, or as congressmen like to say, "codify them into law." Yet, how will the President do it, especially as he is assessing and managing a bureaucracy of over 1.4 million people (*Washington Times*, February 9, 2016), not including military-government employees, many of whom were/are on the other team?

Our President is the Commander-in-Chief of the world's largest military, a force that was neglected and allowed to fall into disarray following years of overuse, and must be quickly strengthened. The turmoil erupting throughout the world forces him to concentrate on foreign affairs while simultaneously trying to deal with domestic issues at home. The first way we can we help our America First agenda go from neutral and through the gears; cruising along towards many big wins down the road for America is by praying.

Think about just a few of the other departments and bureaus that fall under the President's authority such as the EPA, HUD, Treasury, Commerce, Energy, Education, State, Borders, FBI, and the CIA. Most, if not all, are immense, bloated bureaucracies, potentially filled with waste/fraud and distraction and danger. Frankly, I'm overwhelmed at the size of the job. Attempting to efficiently manage an organization as gargantuan as the federal government is unimaginable.

With the immensity of the President's responsibilities in mind, it is good for all of us of the Great Again 63 to pray on behalf of our country, for our President, Congress and yes, for ourselves too. We are, after all, the first and most powerful branch of the four branches: We the People ordained and established the other three.

In the Bible, we are strongly told to "Pray for and give thanks for all men: for all who are in high levels of authority, that we may be blessed to lead tranquil and quiet lives. When we pray this way, it is accepted by God our Savior"
(1 Timothy 2:1-7).

This is especially important when we realize there are those who are actively "praying" just the opposite. Believe it or not, there are covens of witches in America who meet each month to cast a spell of hindrance on President Trump. God's people need to pray in order to counteract their attempts to prevent the president from his goal of restoring America to greatness again (*VOX.com,* October 30, 2017).

Prayer Fuel and a Needed Reaction from God Almighty

Let's pray for our 45th President. Below is just an example of a prayer you could use.

"Lord, we lift up and pray for our President. We thank you for him. We ask that you give him wisdom and strength. He was the man who stepped up willing to fight for America, and you gave him victory in that fight to lead America forward.

Help us to be willing to step up and support him. Show us how to help, how to honor you, how to have your blessing on us once again from sea to sea and from border to border.

You, O God placed him into a role where only you can help him be successful. Help him today at this very moment with all he is doing and all that needs to be done.

May America again be an example to the world of a nation whose God IS the Lord.

Remind him, Lord, to call out to you directly anytime for wisdom. Please give his counselors your unwavering wisdom as they together discuss the great questions and concerns of the day with the President.

Please watch over and bless greatly the Presidents family today. Thank you for all they do to support their father.

Remind us to pray often and spontaneously as needed, knowing with sober awareness that we, our children, and our children's children will be affected by decisions made and actions taken by our President, our Congress and the Supreme Court.

In the name of Jesus Christ we pray, Amen and Amen."

Silent no More

When I think about Trump's description of us as the silent majority, I think it really was an extremely nice, polite way of telling us that the reason we are in the mess we find ourselves in is because we snoozed and allowed much of this political nonsense to occur. Yes, we are the forgotten men and women of America; not only are we forgotten but we forgot our responsibly to participate in our Representative Republic. Not all of us, but many millions of us have shirked this vital responsibility. I want to add that I've been guilty of neglecting my civic duties, too. If you agree with what I'm about to say that's even better, because together perhaps we can clarify as to why we've had such low octane low and power until Trump arrived.

Here it goes: We snoozed, we schmoozed, we boozed, and we stayed in our pews. We prayed, we played, we kicked back, and we had it made. We ignored, we got bored on the shore, and we spent a lot time at the stores buying things we didn't need. We rushed, we wrestled, we tackled and trusted, we invested and digested, we had margaritas and siestas and now we see we came terribly close to being busted, disgusted, and lots of things aren't working; in fact, they are rusted.

Painful description yes, but isn't it true? Or shall we say WAS true-past tense, over and out, end of the line, cease, stopped and dropped. Look straight ahead, neither left nor right; let's keep our focus. Let's resolve again in our heart and head that we, both as individuals and together are going to be involved. We will stay involved and we will make a difference, knowing others will be doing the same. We've got to be Fuel for the Machine once again; good fuel, the right fuel, clean and powerful fuel. Likewise, when the machine is powered by We the People, it will run as it should and in a spectacular manner, thus "Securing the Blessings of Liberty to ourselves and our Posterity."

The Mission Motivation

Your mission, as a former silent agent, should you choose to accept it, is to read the US Constitution. When you do, the first thing you will see is the Preamble. Notice right away those first Fifty-two words and how they clearly identify what our government is supposed to actively pursue and to maintain while it serves us. Here's the preamble:

We the People of the United States, in Order to form a more perfect Union, establish Justice, insure domestic Tranquility, provide for the common defense, promote the general Welfare, and secure the Blessings of Liberty to ourselves and our Posterity, do ordain and establish this Constitution for the United States of America.

Take a moment and write down your thoughts about these words. What do they mean to you and ask yourself if they are being upheld today, focused on, or neglected?

Unity? Justice? Tranquility? Defense? Welfare? Blessings?

United we stand, divided we end up like everyone else with no justice no peace, weakness, unkind and on the wrong side of God. We won't let that happen. We can't let that happen.

Perhaps more than ever before, our President, our nation and our posterity need us to do something we may have never done before. Like Trump, we too need to step up and step into the political arena. We no longer can be shy armchair Americans. We are great again activists standing with our President. His voice is our voice.

"I am never shy about creating news by being controversial and fighting back. Remember, we need to make sure this country stands up and fights back." *Donald Trump* --Crippled America

Just

But…*who are we*… to do such powerful sounding things you ask? After all, we're *just* regular Middle Americans; *just* the bill payers, *just* the war fighters, the Harley riders, the job makers, the workers, nurses, machinists, assemblers, clerks, carpenters, bricklayers, teachers, salespeople, soldiers, managers, *just* regular folks. You know, *just* the silent mass-assive majority.

Who are we?!! The truth is bold and invigorating, drawn from our Declaration of Independence and operating in our Constitution. The declarative theme runs in, through, and behind our Constitution today, exactly like a program installed on a computer or an app for your phone. For example, many people who run a Windows based operating system have no idea that underlying it all is the old DOS system that was first created way back in 1981. DOS is still the foundation for all Windows systems, despite it seeming antiquated, with most Americans having no idea how to use it. It runs behind the scenes. You don't see it unless you need it, wake it up, turn it on, or look for it. Let's take a good look at it once again. Our Declaration is called one of the worlds immortal documents; this is why we celebrate it SO LOUDLY, SO BRIGHTLY, So faithfully every year on July 4th.

Note that we do not celebrate our Constitution or the Bill of Rights in similar fashion because, while very important, they both are simply the armor, helmet and shield over the heart and soul of our liberty and independence. Our Constitution is the blueprint for governance, but the Declaration of Independence is our stated reason for existing. It has been rightly called America's birth certificate.

Read it slowly and drink in the spirit and danger of its propositions. Imagine you are there alongside Jefferson, Hancock, Franklin, Witherspoon, Rodney, John and Samuel Adams. These men, along with their wives and children, were among the Fifty-Six who changed the world by stepping up, fighting back, unafraid of being controversial. Audaciously they stepped up and were willing to risk all during a pivotal time when America was crippled, its people vulnerable, and a deep bureaucracy had overstepped all reasonable boundaries; becoming a serious threat instead of a troublesome servant. Here are the first two paragraphs of this amazing kick in the pants to King Soros. Oops. I mean King George:

In Congress, July 4, 1776

The Unanimous Declaration of the 13 United States of America

"When in the Course of human events, it becomes necessary for one people to dissolve the political bands which have connected them with another, and to assume among the powers of the earth, the separate and equal station to which the Laws of Nature and of Natures God entitle them, a decent respect to the opinions of mankind requires that they should declare the causes which impel them to the separation.

We hold these truths to be self-evident, that all men are created equal, that they are endowed by their Creator with certain unalienable Rights, that among these are Life, Liberty and the pursuit of Happiness.-- That to secure these rights, Governments are instituted among Men, deriving their just powers from the consent of the governed, -that whenever any Form of Government becomes destructive of these ends, it is the Right of the People to alter or to abolish it, and to institute new Government , laying its foundation on such principles and organizing its powers in such form, as to them shall seem most likely to effect their Safety and Happiness."

BOOM!

Signed by the deplorable 56, these "dangerous," thoughtful, intuitive men fueled a movement that God blessed and brought about a change the world had never seen before nor has seen since. This movement that began over two centuries ago continues today, right now, at this very moment. Liberty and limited government are still in style, still cool, and still blessable by God. And just as importantly, still work.

The 56 chose the Great George Washington to lead the battle against the British Deep State, the King's swamp. With his bold warrior leadership, unconventional ways of fighting and with prayer to the sovereign God of the universe, they prevailed against the mightiest military on earth and, as they say …the rest is history.

I think it valuable to read the Declaration in its entirety from time to time, reflecting on the fact that that by affixing their names to it, they were not just exercising their "right to freedom of speech," these 56 signers had committed treason and faced the hangman's noose. Would you have done that? Me? Ehhh, let me think about that.

Notice that it doesn't just go off half-cocked on an emotional rant. Instead, it points the finger at the crown to declare "Facts...of repeated injuries and usurpations." When we read through the list of grievances, it is eerie how many of them seem as if this document could have been produced today against our own federal government. We read of government regulations, taxes, fees, tolls, complicated wasters of our time etc. Hear it in yesterday's vernacular; "erected a multitude of new offices and sent hither swarms of Officers to harass our people and eat out their substance." In the first two paragraphs, take note of several statements directed at the British crown, the legitimate government of their day. Their answers then are our answers today. Check it out.

"Declare the causes" why we are taking over, tossing you and your dangerous policies out. You've abused us and it must and will stop.

"We hold these truths to be self-evident" we can see these truths but you cannot or will not; another reason to toss you and your government.

"Right of the People to alter...abolish...institute new Government" Folks, we can do what we want as long as we continue to hold to the self-evident truths.

"Laying its foundation on...principles...organizing its powers...as to them shall seem...most likely to effect their Safety and Happiness." We have a great foundation. Yes, it is buried, but it is still there and super solid. Our principle objective is to make America great. To do so we will reorganize our government, change its priorities away from itself and back to Justice, domestic tranquility, defense, general welfare and the blessings of liberty to ourselves and our posterity and yes, Americans and America first.

Consider that at the time they all signed the Declaration, the 13 states were vastly outnumbered and severely under financed to wage war against Great Britain, the superpower of the day; yet they prevailed.

And so shall we.

Our Reality Show

We are the Governed. The machine of government forces us to do things, when to do them, and how. I realize this sounds harsh but it's true. The question is, to what degree and to what complexity can they force us to do something or demand something of us, like waste our time, take our money etc?

Reminder: the machine of government, that governs us, needs our very consent to govern us. For our government to run as designed, we must tell it what we want it to do, when we want it to do it, and how we want it done, all within the confines and principles of our Constitution, and with common sense. It also wouldn't hurt us to again embrace the spirit of and safety of the Ten Commandments and the Golden Rule either. Thou shall not steal or lie or kill just might do us some good again or are they considered too out dated? I don't think so.

"Trump is the most dangerous person ever"
---*Head Swampitician of the DNC* (aka Tom Perez)

Wait Tom; do you say that because Trump isn't a politician?

Uh oh. Neither are we so we must be pretty dangerous too.

Perhaps in the same way the supporters of the 56 were dangerous.

Let facts be submitted to a candid world.

Facts are stubborn things.

Especially to Progs like Tom who refuse to recognize them.

BOOM!

Here's a little something to reflect on, all you America First-Great Again activists.

Not one Democrat voted to cut our taxes in 2017. Not One.

Yet all of the Democrats made sure that our tax cuts were only temporary tax cuts. They will expire in 2025.

Democrats would NOT vote for tax cuts and they would not vote to keep our tax cuts permanent.

DUMB!

Chapter Two

The Driver

Qualified

We the American People elected a non-politician to our highest office.

Donald J. Trump, a man who unashamedly vowed to put America first is a man who walked away from a life of phenomenal hand-built luxury. The person in this unfolding non-politician success story is President of The United States of America. President Trump is now the official driver of our executive branch machine and needs us to be the fuel, just as much as we need him in the driver's seat.

I hear an objection.

"But... but... but... he's never held office, he's rich, he's not qualified, he's not "Presidential" enough."

A Few Things about Qualifications

The Left, some Rhinos, and establishment elites continue to try to disqualify Trump with their malarkey and by their feigned ignorance (they aren't ignorant but devious since they also disqualify you, me and our constitutional right to choose any leader we want). The left sees their power quickly slipping away as the light of truth reveals that their short-sighted policies had dangerously eroded and destabilized our nation. Trump has been President for a year. He's had great success. It is even more apparent to Americans now that the left is either incompetent or negligent or both because Trump has done so well in such a short time and did what he promised to do.

This is Brilliant – Let's review

The Progressive left and Mainstream Media Fraud Castors don't want you to know that the exact qualifications for president are brilliantly simple; from the US Constitution Article Two - Section One:

One: The President must be a natural born American citizen.

Two: He must be at least thirty-five years of age.

Three: He must be a resident of the United States for at least fourteen years.

These qualifications are brilliant in that our forefathers did not articulate any particular type of person or skill set or education or wealth for the office of President. This simple brilliance gave the people total responsibility for filling the executive office from the widest selection of Americans. Yes, they built in a few safeguards to prevent a foreign agent from holding the office and they had an almost perfect example to emulate in President George Washington. But they entrusted everyday citizens, each one of us, to choose who should be the head of the country; deciding for ourselves alone if his experience and associations, among other attributes, qualified him for the office.

The three physical qualifications are birthplace, age and residency. If a person meets these, then under the Constitution they are qualified for the office, period. Nowhere does it state anything about previous job experience in government.

So, in light of the three constitutional requirements, let's think a bit about the motives of the Prog left who try to infer that President Trump is unqualified.

I think many, or most, on the Left are misled while claiming we are misled. Okay, stalemate here; except there is one key difference. When we disagree with someone politically, we never violently riot, harm, encourage others to kill, or destroy things because we don't agree with their heroes, Presidents Obama and Clinton or Jimmy Carter. And we never will.

In fact, it has been noted that when the Left finishes some type of meeting or gathering, they often leave the place in total disarray with trash and garbage everywhere, including human waste. Yet, Tea Party and Right to Life groups are known for always leaving a place as clean as or cleaner than before they came. This contrast reveals a great deal about how each group respects other people, especially the "little guy" who has to clean up after them.

Grossly misled, the Progs obviously intend to continuously belittle President Trump and our America First agenda throughout his terms as president. Those who believe in big government/world government will constantly work to blunt the Great Again agenda for the entire eight years he holds the office, but they will fail.

Blunters

Their motive is to blunt, stall, and damage his reform agenda by magnifying manufactured controversies through idle speculation, using their allies in the media who bring their personal biased opinions to their reporting; and let's not forget those "unnamed sources." They are relentless in this area, even if it means making up fake news; news not intended to inform us but to deform our America First agenda. Yes, we're talking about Fraud Castors, Inc.

Prog journalists intend to deconstruct the rare and opulent example we now have of a successful citizen non-politician who brought commonsense Middle American-style reasoning into the White House. What is ironic, is they used to embrace the concept that one of the great things about America is that "anyone can be president" (Anyone except Trump apparently).

They still can't believe it has happened and they never want to see it happen again, which further explains the intensity and pounding they serve up against President Trump every day, even when he does something few presidents do. For example, following Hurricane Harvey devastating Houston, he announced he was giving a million dollars of his own money to help the victims. Instead of being congratulated for his example, he was condemned by celebrities who bragged about raising a greater amount of money, while neglecting to note it was other people's money they were donating, not much of their own.

However, as we have repeatedly seen, not only can the president take a pounding, he can give as good as he gets. When was the last time you saw that flavor on the national stage, perhaps in Rocky or Defiance or in The Shawshank Redemption. With his bravery, guts, and sharp political instincts, he chooses to fight for America. Just as a general cannot fight a war alone and a NASCAR driver must have a pit crew, we too must step up, pitch in, and help out.

His attitude reminds me of the very pointed response he gave at a campaign rally after HRC wanted all her supporters to pledge that they were somehow "with her." Trump said:

"I chose to recite a different pledge. My pledge reads: I'm with you, the American people. I am your voice. So, to every parent who dreams for their child and every child who dreams of their future, I say these words to you tonight. I am with you. I will fight for you. And I will win for you."

Bravo, Mr. President. A promise made and a promise we see being kept every single day. Thank you for fighting and winning for us.

"To avoid criticism, say nothing, do nothing, be nothing." --*Socrates*

"Let him who would move the world first move himself." --*Socrates*

New Driver Heard Something that Didn't Sound Good

A good driver who knows vehicles can detect when something is wrong just by the sound of the engine or the vibes through the steering wheel. He compares what he hears now to his past experience of how it ideally should sound or feel. Donald Trump reacted to the sound of a government machine that had long failed to defend our national and personal interests. The machine was in serious need of repair.

The president brought a fresh perspective when he looked over the machine before deciding to be a candidate. Upon inspection, he didn't like what he heard and how the vehicle was being driven.

Summary: Donald J. Trump's Presidential Announcement in June 2016

"We don't have victories anymore."

"The US has become a dumping ground for everybody else's problems."

"We have no protection, no competence. We don't know what's happening."

"Our enemies are getting stronger and we are getting weaker."

"How stupid are our leaders? We have all the cards but don't know how to use them."

"We are tired of being ripped off; we are becoming a third world country."

He reacted to all of these problems, not by just griping about it like many do, but by doing something about it. Rather than get others to pony up for his campaign, who would expect something in return, he put his money where his mouth is; running a campaign that ignored the sterile, predictable, political science methods and reached out directly to really good hardworking and forgotten people. People he knew instinctively were busy, silent, distracted and just tired of losing; tired of being ignored, tired of political frauds. People living life while big problems continued to creep up on them. Yes, Trump reacted; he did something great and he cared.

"I couldn't stand to see what was happening to our great country. This mess calls for leadership in the worst way." Crippled America -- *Donald J Trump*

The Right Fuel, Periodic Maintenance, the Right Driver

Vehicles are created to run on certain types of fuel specific to them. An automobile runs on gasoline with 85 octane, a racing car with 110 octane. A semi-truck runs on diesel and a Marine fighter jet runs on JP-5. But what happens when the wrong fuel is placed in a vehicle?

Obviously BIG TROUBLE!!

If any vehicle is powered by the wrong fuel, the results are catastrophic. The jet crashes, the tractor can't plow, the dragster won't jump off the line, the racecar loses its exceptional speed, and the rocket won't lift off.

When bad fuel is poured into the government machine we all lose. We lose our freedom, our basic rights are jeopardized, we lose control, we crash, we dive, we get stuck, we get weakened, we become vulnerable and exposed. Everyone in the Middle is especially vulnerable. Society becomes unstable. Are we there yet? We were close.

"There are only two times to do something: now and too late." --*unknown*

"A knot doesn't untie itself." --*unknown*

Do the words vulnerable and unstable accurately describe where you think America is at this point in history, even with our brave and courageous 45th President in the driver's seat? Together, we'll help him get this thing back on track, with its wheels travelling within the grooves of the Constitution. But it has taken decades to get here and it'll take many years to get out.

Is this Thing running as it should?

A few months back, I hopped into my son's 17-year-old car. It's a great old vehicle. It's well made and the previous owner took great care of it. As I started driving, I heard an unusual sound that made me perk up and listen intently. When I took it out on the road I grew very concerned. It was really loud and I determined it was either a bad tire or a bad front wheel bearing. Backing off on the speed, I carefully drove the car home. Upon further inspection, it was the wheel bearing which fell apart when I later removed it. If this had failed at a high rate of speed in heavy traffic, the results could have been disastrous. The entire wheel could have come off, potentially causing a multi-car pileup. The sound was so unusual and obvious to me that I wondered why my son didn't tell me about it.

When I talked with him I learned a couple of basic things about human nature.

One, he always has music on and plays it rather loudly while he drives. So the dull roar of the bad bearing was covered up by "The Red Jumpsuit Apparatus" and "Owl City" as he merrily rolled along. ♪La La La La♫. If he had heard it, it would be easy to dismiss it as an issue with the road rather than the car.

Second, the bearing didn't go bad overnight. It generally takes several months between the time a wheel bearing first loses its seal and lubricant until each metal bearing pin is dry. The friction then becomes great enough to produce intense heat generated by the weight of the vehicle which starts producing a really bad grinding rumbling sound leading up to mechanical breakdown and failure.

When the bearing first started to fail, it barely made any noticeable sound. But because of use, gradually over time, the problem became worse until it became the really bad sound I'd heard. It was a pronounced event that to me was obvious that something was not normal, but my son had tuned it out, inadvertently covering it up and he had gotten used to it; like a person living by a railroad track not hearing when a train comes by at 3:45 every night. He is also a very busy young guy and as a result of all these things, the problem crept up on him as he was living life. Just normal stuff.

I, on the other hand, due to my experience, reacted to the sound and did something about it because I love the kid and always want him to be as safe as possible.

Likewise, Trump reacted to the sound of a mismanaged government that had and still has many serious issues. Because of his love of people and for our country, he decided it was time to jump in and fix the problems. Breakdown and failure were not an option; the problems could no longer be ignored.

Here is a wise quote to let slosh around your think tank:

"The masses never revolt of their own accord, and never revolt merely because they are oppressed. Indeed, so long as they are not permitted to have standards of comparison, they never even become aware that they are oppressed." *--George Orwell, 1984*

Like my son, Americans were busy, distracted and we just got used to the sound and look of a mismanaged government. We really had nothing in recent memory to compare it to. Just normal stuff.

Convertibles and Hardtops

Can or will skeptical anti-Trumpsters be converted, so to speak, in the future? You know, metaphorically rolling back the hardtop to allow the refreshing wind of independent thought to clear the mind, heart and soul of the dark constraints that hide the truth? Will they soon realize they are simply parroting ideas meant to conform, even program them; resisting what could be a modern new birth of American freedom, filled with endless opportunities for them?

Maybe that describes someone you know. Maybe that was you at one time or that's you right now.

A hardtop doesn't allow one to look up and see beyond the ceiling of the car. This visibility restriction is self-imposed but predictably safe. You'll never be sunburned or caught in the rain, but it's dull.

I have hope that with a bit of study, any skeptic that honestly examines America's foundational period of history will be greatly enthused with the founders' vision for our great unlimited potential, elaborated in our Declaration as: Life, Liberty and the Pursuit of Happiness.

The President gives a parallel supporting message whenever he says, "We Will Make America Great Again;" essentially by limiting the government that has limited us for far too long. Liberty for us-limits for our government. We are the change and yes we are and must be the chains too.

"In questions of power then let no more be heard of confidence in man, but bind him down from mischief by the chains of the Constitution." --*Thomas Jefferson*

The drivers we fired are screaming that Trump doesn't have the proper training or experience to operate or drive our machine. I bet they'll repeat and parrot this nonsense for years.

Did you hear it too?

Trump doesn't have the proper training.

Trump doesn't have the experience required.

Trump doesn't know government.

OH??

We are the People.

We own this machine.

We inherited it from our wise and brave forefathers.

We validate our new driver. Not them. Thank God.

We trust this driver more than any driver we have had in a long, long time. Yes, we BELIEVE what he says because he thinks like US. He is one of us, not one of the political ruling classes.

You see, when we interviewed him we found...

He has heart; the heart of a lion.

He has common sense.

He sounds a lot like the drivers we had many years ago, back when America was great.

So here's the way it is.

He has our authority to operate our machine, and SINCE WE OWN THIS MACHINE, we certify him as being qualified to drive it. Not only that, we want him to drive it the way it was originally designed: for Americans on the American track.

Previous drivers took the liberty of taking our machine down roads it wasn't built for; using it for things it wasn't intended to be used. They were hauling loads beyond its capacity, hitting things, leaving road kill, and often polluting where it went. It hasn't won a trophy in so long that most fans thought it was disqualified or sitting in a junkyard somewhere.

You get the point; extreme neglect, terrible drivers, very little maintenance, and bad fuels have all but destroyed this vehicle unless she gets some major TLC. That's where WE step in. We are going to change things; we are going to the races for the ride of our lives! Yee Haw!

The blue-collar billionaire deserves our Middle American blue-collar prayers, allegiance, alliance and our Fuel.

High horsepower machines are equipped with Super Turbo chargers that increase the fuel volume, adding a huge boost of power to the machine. Our machine must be equipped with a super charged Super Majority, committed to accomplishing Great Things with our President. We are also the equippers of the congressional machine. In years 2018-20-22-24 we must be ready for the primary elimination rounds. These are hot races but at lower speeds, this is why it is very important to knock out the compromising Progs or any middle road moderates before they make it into the bigger races.

A Spiritual Rest Stop

I have hope that anyone reading through this book will discover, as I have, that the God of our Fathers can free anyone from any and all dark conformity that limits their life potential.

There is nothing better than to look up and see further ahead as you ride on the road of life blessed, free and as a happy person.

I pray that if you don't know what salvation in Christ Jesus is, that you will let this rest stop be a nugget that you'll want to pull over and closely examine for yourself.

Perhaps start by verbally asking for God's help as you look into this stuff if it's new to you or seems a bit weird.

Here is how Jesus explained it to Paul the apostle after Paul had his eyes opened: **"...Now I send you, to open their eyes, that they may turn from darkness to light and from the power of Satan unto God, that they may receive forgiveness of sins, and an inheritance among those who are sanctified by faith in me"** (Acts 26:18).

I can't fully explain to you how amazing it was to learn that **"God so loved the world that he gave his one and only Son that whoever believes in him should not perish, but have eternal life"** (John 3:16).

It's your choice to either roll back the spiritual hardtop or continue driving with self-imposed limitations. Honestly, you have nothing to lose and everything to gain. Be Free and ride in the light with the refreshing wind of Christ blowing into your soul, for he is the real basis of life, liberty, and the pursuit of happiness.

What is he talking about and why?

You might be wondering what in the world does this have to do with the qualifications for president. Good question and here is the answer.

Just as there are very minimal qualifications imposed on any candidate to become president (birthplace, age and residency), God likewise imposes very minimal qualifications on any person who wants his inheritance, wants his forgiveness, and wants eternal life.

The qualifications God places on mankind are beautiful and simple: **"If you confess with your mouth that Jesus is Lord, and believe in your heart that God raised him from the dead, you will be saved."** These qualifications are from Romans 10:9. Confess and believe. BOOM! Now we are talking freedom here. Real freedom.

As for the inheritance, we do very little to become his child except to confess and believe in the birth, death, and resurrection of Jesus (Gods only Son). Not only do we get a future inheritance, we get the blessings of an abundant life here and now, filled with peace and complete forgiveness for every single wrong we ever did or will do. Later, when we breathe our last breath, we are welcomed home to heaven which is designed and hand built by the Father and his carpenter son, Jesus. How cool is that? A world where we belong and we are told it's a place with no tears, no pain, and definitely no political parties. Woo Hoo!

Weeds

Politics and life in general are so cool, so exciting, yet can also be so overwhelming, complicated, and uncertain. Our many challenges and problems today have a root source or a "cause" and that cause has produced consequences; ones that we continue to see and feel the brunt of today. For myself, this cause and effect explanation helps me to understand calmly and objectively why we are facing what we face and more importantly how to address the mess we are in. I hope this cause and effect explanation will help you as well.

Adam, the first man, was given an instruction by God to not eat of the tree of the knowledge of good and evil. He was told that the day he did, he would die. Read Genesis 1-3 for the account. Adam disobeyed. Rather than admit his mistake, he blamed his wife and God. Because he disobeyed (the cause), he and all mankind now toil where there once was ease; instead of an unlimited life span, he and all of his posterity would eventually die, that's us too (the effect). Where food was once easy to plant and harvest, we now must toil with thorns and thistles (another effect). In the environment of not following Gods instruction, crime sprung up very quickly with one son killing his brother due to jealousy. Man, did he blow it for his family and for the rest of us or what? Then came regulations, taxes and…just kidding (kind of).

I view the mess America is in today as the continuation of the thorns, thistles, weeds, and the consequences passed down to us from the first man. Like thorns and thistles, problems continually spring up, seemingly from nowhere, and are impossible to fully eradicate. A thorn in your finger or foot is painful, thistle weed chokes out vital crops, and let's not forget that nasty natural irritant good old *toxicodendron radican*, aka poison ivy. Mankind's problems hurt, harm, irritate, and limit life in America. Yes, we recognize things are much worse in other parts of the world but the U.S. is traveling the same road. We can see the malignant weed effect all around us, can't we? If we ignore the source we end up blaming and fighting each other instead of doing the right things together with unity. The Great Again agenda provides both the plan and the unity to be Great Again together.

Just like Adam, our messes today have at their source, disobedience to God. In a nutshell, we have the Bible, the instruction manual for life. However we chose to ignore much of what it says, preferring instead to do things our own way. You may find this surprising, but that's fine with God.

God always, by grace and mercy, allows mankind to exercise our free will; not forcing anything on us except to allow the consequences, and even those are meant to teach and give us wisdom to do things differently. Our mistakes help turn us back to God to get us back to what has worked, what has blessed, and what kept the thorns and thistles under control. America's founders knew this and put safeguards in place to help us fight back against the thorns and thistles and keep them at bay.

We've strayed from our founding principles and are suffering with thorns and thistles. Pain, limited growth, conflict, disunity, crime, insolvency and more are self-evident.

This is kind of like first hearing crickets at night or a front wheel bearing; it's an awareness thing, a comparison thing.

Awareness, sobriety, observation; all describe senses that are natural and can be improved upon. Let's use all that we have to help America seek Almighty God again. That too would be great!

Our Roles in the Garden of America

If we compare planting a garden to rediscovering our own roles in the garden of American freedom, we realize that we have work to do. Once thorns and thistles are yanked out, we till the ground, add the seed, add some fertilizer, once God blesses with sufficient rainfall, we should get some good crops for our efforts. While this formula works, removal of weeds from a garden is never a one-time thing. No matter how hard we try to keep the garden weeded, weeds always find a way to return due to dormant hidden seed or unwanted seed brought in from other sources, such as animals or the wind. Likewise, as the saying goes, **the price of freedom is eternal vigilance.**

To keep the field of freedom and liberty cleared of dangerous weedy growths, we must stay vigilant; watch for possible danger. The questions to ask ourselves: have we been watching and have we been vigilant? Have we compared what we were to who we are? With our government, as with a garden, we mustn't get stressed out or paranoid, watching for thorns and thistles every day. But periodic checks every so often as needed and yanking a few out i.e. telling our reps to yank as well will certainly help. Remember, there are 63 million of us tending this baby and our voices, our letters, and our votes are the best weed killer there is.

What does all this have to do with fuel? Well, by removing contaminated policies and the elected public officials that spread them, we will ensure that a better crop is produced whenever we follow the manual of our great Constitution; just as in our metaphorical example, bad fuel results in the poor performance of any machine.

Smothered by Big Brother

"The most effective way to destroy people is to deny and obliterate their own understanding of their history." *George Orwell*

Because nature is such a great teacher, check out Psalm 19 and Romans 1:19-20 to see why nature is absolutely amazing or just gaze out of the window or up at the stars.

Let's start with the awesome word liberty. At first you might associate it with left-wing liberals who support big government and support expansive welfare programs. The reality is, liberty is an old word that has nothing to do with this, and frankly it is not well understood by us today.

This is probably due to our system of government-controlled education: mandated, cleverly and heavily controlled. It is called manipulation, which extracts or smothers most anything that has to do with our founding. Here is a test to see if it worked: What was the motto of Americas Revolutionary War? Do you know? Did you ever know?

The Motto: "No King But King Jesus". Surprised? So was I!

This smothering has pretty much affected the teaching about how every American has a responsibility to secure the "Blessings of Liberty" that our founders put in our Constitution as something that should be the natural outgrowth of a representative people-powered government. "Give me liberty or give me death," Patrick Henry powerfully said.

"If liberty means anything at all it means the right to tell people what they do not want to hear." --*George Orwell*

Of course, we can't talk about liberty without looking to the Great author of the Declaration of Independence and the Virginia Statute of Religious Liberty:

"Rightful Liberty is unobstructed action according to our will within the limits drawn around us by the equal rights of others. I do not add 'within the limits of the law' because law is often but the tyrants will, and always so when it violates the rights of the individual."--*Thomas Jefferson*

Our role today is to fan the embers of liberty; adding oxygen (fuel!) once again to secure the blessings of American liberty. Picture liberty this way: a glowing ember smothered under a mountain of wet leaves. What do the leaves represent? Taxes, fees, regulations, political correctness, elite entrenched establishment politicians and their special interests, wasteful government spending, globalist wealth/job redistribution, long and questionable wars, open borders, drug smuggling, banned prayer, abortion, sex slavery, banned Ten Commandments, sanctuary cities etc.

The fire of liberty won't go out completely so long as people like us know it still glows and is rekindable (guess that makes us the kindling) once it's stoked up has unlimited potential for greatness. Thanks to Trump, we were reminded that liberty is indeed there and it, as well as ourselves, were and are being smothered by a government that not only has the ability to give everything to us (until it or we the people go bankrupt), but also has the power to take everything from us. That I guess is defined as a massive conundrum.

Keeping the pile of smothering leaves concept, let's revisit Orwell's quote: **Indeed, so long as they are not permitted to have standards of comparison, they never even become aware that they are oppressed."**

Until people were permitted "standards of comparison," we were oblivious to any real substantive choice out there in political candidate land.

Trump Changed Everything

During the primaries and general elections, We the People had the opportunity to compare Trump against the other candidates and we revolted against the political engineers, many who had a hand in creating the deep mess we find ourselves in as a nation. And it is a deep mess; a really deep mess indeed, a mountain of a mess, a deep state mount ton of mess.

We can no longer ignore the mess or the deep state usurpers who helped create it and seek to continue it at our peril, and were poised to grow the freaking thing even bigger.

The result would be that the troublesome servant would indeed have become the fearful master Washington warned us about.

Americans lose when our history and former standards remain smothered i.e. Biblical liberty, Constitutional liberty, entrepreneurial liberty, common sense, independence, and educational integrity. All of these are proven standards that once produced both a limited government and an unlimited free and safe people; all in a society awash in unity, justice, tranquility and prosperity. We once were (think of the greatest generation) a great nation that had secured the blessings of Liberty greater than any other nation before or since and until we do so again, we as a society will end up with the fearful master over us; cowering as we beg for a piece of our own bread while leaving us vulnerable and exposed to multiple dangers. Wasn't that the path we were on the past eight-plus years before Trump?

With Trump we can tame the fearful master.

With God we get back to Great.

Below is part of the First Prayer of the Continental Congress, 1774 by Reverend Jacob Duche. Get and read the entire prayer. You'll notice it was answered in full 100%.

"Oh Lord our Heavenly Father, high and mighty King of kings, and Lord of lords, who from thy throne behold all the dwellers on earth and reigns with power supreme and uncontrolled over all the Kingdoms, Empires and Governments; look down in mercy, we beseech Thee, on these our American states, who have fled to Thee from the rod of the oppressor and thrown themselves on Thy gracious protection, desiring to be henceforth dependent only on Thee."

Chapter Three

The Obvious

Trump, with his amazing common sense instincts, continually points out the troubling policy mistakes of the previous administration(s) such as the Iranian/arm-your-enemy mistake, the Obamacare/take-one-sixth-of-the-economy-for-healthcare-but-not-know-what-you-are-doing mistake, the $7 billion ineffectively spent on air-traffic-control to-slightly-improve-it plan or the $2.1 billion spent on the website healthcare.gov, built by an Obama administration friend that was so awful it was the butt of numerous jokes. But still *Mess Mountain* remains curiously "invisible" to the Left and yet there's so much more to see. Trump saw it, showed it to us and the left is not happy that he has. Too bad.

Under President Obama's and Hillary Clinton's watch, twenty percent of America's uranium was sold to a Canadian firm who then sold it to the "friendly" 4,300 nuclear-missiles aimed-directly-at-us Russian government.

By sheer coincidence, shortly thereafter, the Canadian middleman just happened to follow up with a $145 million donation to the Clinton Foundation. Then another coincidence, Bill Clinton is invited to speak in Russia, pocketing an impressive $500,000 fee from Putin for his service. Source: WND.com 4/23/17.

How did Trump's Russian "collusion" do all that? He must be the greatest bungler that ever lived, because most collaborators do things to help each other, not their opponents.

Great Again Attention Needed Folks and Needed Now

Ironic but to compare and contrast this Clinton/Obama/Russian slick stuff, think about when an older

American on social security earns just a few thousand extra dollars. They end up pummeled with taxes and could lose some of their S.S. income.

This is plain wrong.

Something needs to be done about both.

One is lawless abuse times ten, the other...enslavement by the system.

One grossly unregulated, the other grossly over regulated.

One group has jeopardized national security while retired seniors are chained to regulation, restricted and threatened by a system they paid into, they own, and they rely on. The establishment plays pals with our enemies but seems openly hostile to our own people; if they move just a bit to help themselves they get zapped. That is C- Rap.

When someone retires at 62-70 years old, government should give them their retirement income and leave them the heck alone. SS income should be a no strings attached, keep-your-nose-out-of-our-lives American benefit for years worked. Period. Let's make that happen. Fuel the idea.

Congress wastes a lot of our money. It takes money from us and redistributes it to bottomless pits. This occurs every day in America.

Don't just take my word for it, you can read about $85 billion worth of examples of this outrageous negligence in "Waste Watch" document #4 which you can see at Congressman Steve Russell's web site:

http://www.Russell.house.gov/wastewatch

It is bizarre that $85,000,000,000-emphasis BILLIONS-are handed out/spent and wasted by apparently unaccountable people with full approval of our Congressional leaders.

To put $85 billion into real-life context so we could understand how much it is, I divided it by 52 weeks. That gave me an amount of $1,634,615,384 wasted (that's 1.6 billion) every week which comes to $233,516,483 (that's 233 millions) wasted every single day.

That comes to $9,729,853 (that's only $10 million/chump change) every hour, everyday all year long year after year after year. Number 9 number 9 number 9…

$162,164 per minute!!

If we hired and paid people $90,000 a year each to work on any project you could think of, we could hire 2,594 people a DAY every Day for a year with this amount of money. With $85 billion, we could hire 946,800 people to work for one year and pay them $90,000 each.

Congressman Russell has seven waste watch documents for you to see on his web site and this $85 billion is only the tip of a few icebergs.

Another thing we could do is divide the $85 billion between all of the 138 million taxpayers and cut each of them a $615 check every year. Or how about this idea; we randomly select from the social security roster 233 retired Americans every day and award each of them 1 million dollars. The only stipulation being they must spend half of it over the course of one year. America would have 85,045 seniors spending our money every year. I bet they'd do a great job spending it. Crazy idea? No crazier than what is going on now.

There are a few sites for you to look at with other examples you can read about and use when you call or write your representative and senator. The sites I've listed below contain more factual information that we can use to demand an end to this mishandling of our money. I'm sure once you look at some of the **"mishandling**," a few different words will come to mind such as **highway robbery**-theft-**negligence**-malfeasance-**disgusting**-stupid-**bribery**-payoffs-**kickbacks**-asleep at the switch-**asinine**-dereliction of duty-**crazy-blind-drunk.**

Congressman Ken Buck has a great book that explains the back story of what goes on in D C. It is entitled "Drain the Swamp: How Washington corruption is worse than you think." Read it, run for office and stand with Ken. If Maxi, Nancy, Steny, and Bernie can win, so can you. Believe it.

No Sense

Keep in mind that even though this wasteful spending makes little sense or is outrageous to us, it actually represents FORCE and POWER, which helps RE-ELECTION, and raises CONTRIBUTIONS, providing CONTROL in their/our districts by the amount of bacon they bring home and gives FAVOR with other reps and EMPLOYMENT to special persons within their districts. All of which leads to RE-ELECTION and POWER and FORCE, perpetuating the cycle and growing the mess mount ton.

Remember Washington's definition: *"Government is not reason, it is not eloquence, it is force."* Yes, even when you're a senior having contributed your entire life to the nation they limit and force you to do what they will not do. We all will be old someday and must force our government to serve us, not limit us. Make Americans first Again!

Think: when just a little more than half of the Congress, a majority, claim they want to stop wasteful spending, we still keep over spending. Hmmm.

Here are the additional sites to more fully understand the scope of wasteful congressional spending.

Openthebooks.com an awesome site

cagw.org see their critical waste issues

Heritage.org see their budget and spending pages.

federalbudgetinpictures.com

Lankford.senate.gov/fumbles

judicialwatch.org

These sites will infuriate you. All are put up by great folks that seem to be either conservative and/or Republican. They are definitely with us to help us fuel the machine's new direction through contact with our reps.

I must ask, what is it about most Democrats and many Republicans that make them think they can simply ignore the financial jeopardy they have put us in? The gross over regulation they have us under? Their silence and their resistance, especially to spending cuts, show us exactly who they care about, and it doesn't seem to be us or our posterity. Where are their websites showing overspending and bloated department budgets filled with non-essential spending?

Obvious

In light of the wasteful spending let's ask a couple of pointed questions: Would it be better to cut billions in waste and use the savings to pay down the debt, enabling us to pay less interest to China, Japan, the Cayman Islands, Ireland, Brazil, Switzerland, the United Kingdom, Hong Kong and Taiwan? Interest payments on US debt will rise from $250 billion in 2017 to $770 billion in 2027. We are definitely going in the wrong direction. Source: **federalbudgetinpictures.com**

Is it ironic to you that Congress spent this money so wastefully while gutting our military? Our forces didn't get pay raises, and our seniors' social security didn't see an increase in their monthly budget while these other wasteful departments did. Fortunately for members of our military, President Trump did get their pay increased not long after storming the White House.

Why can't we cut spending across the board by 5% from every part of government except our military? That's five bucks out of every hundred dollars. Why won't Congress simply do that? If we look back to the $85 billion they wasted and cut just 5% that would only amount to $4.25 billion, still leaving them $81 billion to waste.

I bet we Americans lost more than 5% of our jobs or 5% of our investments during the last recession, which supposedly ended just a few months after President Obama took office; or lost 5% or more of our income due to increases in food, fuel, transportation, insurance hikes, healthcare costs, college tuition hikes, property tax increases, utility hikes, or red tape regulations. We should force them to cut at least 5% now. With a $20 trillion debt, how can we be spending what we don't have anyway?

Let's call it the 5% plan. 63 million of us could get it done in a week if we tried, couldn't we? You better believe it!

On that subject, there is in Congress today a plan that balances the federal budget in five years by cutting just one penny out of every dollar the government spends. The "Penny Plan" would balance the budget in five years with a 1% cut. So it would certainly balance in one year with a 5% cut. Yet nothing gets done! They will not cut 1 penny from each dollar. Yet families and seniors are forced to cut much more, pay much more, and scrimp much more.

The President can definitely read a balance sheet and financial statements. He understands that due diligence requires him and his department secretaries to root out waste. Congressmen from both parties know that a businessman armed with common sense, whose priority and allegiance is with the people who pay for government, will find a mountain of waste. He will get a ton of resistance and he has from day one. Prepare for more.

Therein lays our problem, for when Trump exposes all the crazy programs they have thrown money at, they'll lose their power. They will be exposed for supporting ridiculous wasteful spending. Most are Democrats but there are a good number of Republicans as well. It is up to us to be vigilant and diligent to help the president stop this outrageous wasteful spending and return to a policy of good stewardship. We know the trajectory we are on is not sustainable and what is needed is a hard right fiscal turn to put us back onto a sensible path so the machine is less likely to crash from lack of cash.

Our people-powered machine, our representative republic, is not broken. For decades, we have allowed the machine to be driven by a few careless, feckless, even reckless drivers. Others filled the gas tank with toxic, weak and foreign, even exotic fuels.

Yes, it has fallen into some disrepair after 240 years. But no matter what was done to it, it's an enduring machine. Just read the manual again and you will find that it is easily repaired, so long as we schedule ourselves a little time to maintain it, and do it together united.

Hear now from the chief architect of our machine:

"The powers delegated by the proposed Constitution to the Federal government are few and defined. Those which are to remain in state governments are numerous and

indefinite."--*James Madison,* 4th President of the United States

Few and defined, few and defined, few and defined.

Does this sound idealistic? Yes. Is it a standard we could strive for and certainly return to? Absolutely!

No, the left isn't fair, it isn't "bipartisan" (not that bipartisanism is all that good for America-think NAFTA). The Prog Left definitely doesn't want Middle Americans too involved in **our** government either, but you've probably noticed that by now. Scrutiny of the budget or questioning their reasons for spending our money or borrowing money from communist nations is simply none of our business. No, they won't say it to your face but it is self evident as well. Just check out the above web sites to see how they've cleverly hidden how much is spent or what we get for our investment.

For example: from **openthebooks.com** we see that 67 non military agencies of the federal government (far more than a few and never defined) "after grabbing massive legal powers are amassing fire power." They connect their statement to the fact that over an 8 year period these agencies spent $1.5 billion on guns and ammo; the IRS itself buying an unprecedented $13.2 million worth of guns and ammo for itself. What for? Are there shoot outs over why 1040EZ isn't all that easy?

Switch Gears

If Progs ever got their way and somehow changed the constitutional requirements for being president, we could end up with a choice between Ivy League political science attorney, elitist, globalist number one or Ivy League political science attorney, elitist, globalist number two, which really is no choice at all. We saw this with Clinton/Gore, Obama/Biden, and Hillary with old what's-his-name Kane.

With little to choose from, we would be forced to hold our nose and vote for the least offensive of the bunch. Many people would choose to not vote at all, thereby doing exactly what was scripted for them to do by those clever political operatives who use the "science" of politics to manipulate the masses and keep us divided into separate groups or "classes". A short definition for politics is: "The art of gaining power." Budgets are power.

This was the set up and the potentially rigged outcome we faced in 2016, had it come down to a race between Clinton and Bush or Kasich, thus guaranteeing as president either establishment swampitician insider "A" or insider "B," both of whom offered little but to *maybe* sustain the status of a nation in decline or make it worse. Someone has said that the primary difference today between the two parties is that under Democrats, America goes to hell at 100 mile an hour, while under Republicans she only goes there at 60 mph.

Ladies and gents of the great grand election jury, We the People chose neither option A or B.

Drama Rama

After a few impressive warm up laps during the run-up to January 20th, Trump came off the starting line with the pedal to the metal. He shifted into high gear, high RPM, full torque nitro mix, moving powerfully down the track.

Just for fun, pinch your nose and announce in your best Howard Cosell voice:

"To the great horror, annoyance, and numbed shock of everyone on the left, Middle Americans have chosen Donald J. Trump to be the designated driver of the federal machine. As you know, the stockholders of Middle America picked Trump from a crowded field of contenders, choosing him over a large number of veteran drivers. Trump proved to be an aggressive contender and now is poised to change history and the way future races are run. As a reminder, today's race is one of grueling endurance, pitting driver and machine against harsh hazardous conditions during a multi-mile, several year race. This race can be compared to a combination of races like Pikes Peak with its sharp dangerous mountain curves and the Baja 1000, whose spectators actually booby-trap the race course, and the Daytona 500, with very high speeds and the biggest CASH purse of all races. To his credit, Trump has one of the best pit crews ever assembled helping him, and they are committed to his victory. Trump's loyal fans and supporters are huge: 100 percent committed and their numbers are growing quickly. I've never seen anything like it."

(Pause)… "Folks, I see the green flag lowered; and they're off. Trump leaps forward and so begins the race to win back the trophy of limited government and common sense. Trump's racing strategy is to quickly put America first with a series of high speed lane changes followed by bursts of power, leaving the competition in the dust. The crowd goes wild, the media faints, and the establishment is enraged. It's a great day in America!"

The fun has begun! "Few and defined" is coming back in style, Mr. Madison.

President Trump immediately pulled far ahead of the other drivers with his energy and workaholic habits, blended with inventiveness, creativity, and his unique style. With speed, strength, and determination, he did more in the first year than most any President has ever accomplished. Graciously, he reached out to forgotten Americans, even liberals and forgotten allies alike, all the while chopping complicated and limiting regulations with a Congress that hasn't had an ally in the White House for many years. As the beginning of his second year in office comes into view, the President's momentum and skills have increased. He superbly handled several hurricanes, forest fires, and a mass domestic terrorist attack in Las Vegas. Rallies, his first United Nations speech, foreign visits - all were home runs. North Korea and Iran are on notice and ISIS is on the ropes. Enemies from terror nations are no longer permitted free rein and illegal alien gangs are broken up and being removed from the country. Wins in the rear-view mirror are great to look back on and more to see up ahead.

One of the best wins was when the president quickly nominated and seated Judge Neil Gorsuch to the Supreme Court. Judge Gorsuch is touted as a strict Constitutionalist, one who hopefully will balance the court's power and help guide it back to a path that leads to a Federal government whose powers are indeed "few and defined."

As for the Progs, well they remain outraged and in shocked denial, reminding me of someone who'd been tased. Let's stop here for just a second and imagine – Schumer, Warren, Schiff, Maxine, Steny and Nancy – The Trump win still at this late date has them all tasered, so to speak, and still lying on the ground, twitching in disbelief and whining "Why, Who, H... Ha... How did Trump get here? This can't be happening; we don't deserve this, Noooo! Mommy!" "They seem to suck their thumbs in wonder that Trump came in through the bathroom window." A big surprise for them and a dream come true for us.

They act in a manner worthy of Dick Dastardly and his dog Muttley in Wacky Races. Then they utter that famous expression when things don't go their way, "Drat! Drat! And double Drat!" Meanwhile Muttley covers his mouth and snickers with that high-pitched laugh.

To the Prog left, we say: your gig is up. We the People did this, we tased you and the other misguided Swampiticians for ruling as socialists, for empowering bureaucrats, and for listening to globalists, for leaving America vulnerable in many ways, physically and spiritually. We WANT a nation Under God, not a nation under your confused and misguided policies. Frankly, we have just begun. Every two years we will make gains to reclaim our rights and return to Greatness Again.

Isn't this Weird?

Government doesn't know the number of people employed… in our own government!

Today, no one can say with complete authority how many federal agencies exist, or how many work in them. Yet come payday, they all manage to somehow get a check.

The Competitive Enterprise Institute, in an August 26, 2015 article revealed that the number fluctuates wildly, depending on who is asked, from 60 agencies and sub-agencies to 430. A senator from the Senate Judiciary committee said, "The Federal Register indicates there are OVER 430 departments, agencies and sub-agencies in the federal government." The online Federal Register Index depicts 257.

The CEI report goes on to say, "If nobody knows how many agencies exist whose decrees we must abide, that means we don't know how many people work for the government (let alone contractors making a living from taxpayers), nor know how many rules there are. But even if we isolate a given knowable agency, the rise of "regulatory dark matter" may make it hard to tell exactly what is and what is not a rule."

Complicate the simple yet again.

A September 8, 2015 CNS News article has the number of Federal, State and local government employees at 21,995,000. Contrast this number to private sector manufacturing employees at only 12,329,000.

They tell us there are only 7 to 11 million illegal aliens in the country. Some estimates range from Senator Cottons 24 million to as high as 40 million, no one knows. This proves Trump's point about incompetency at every level.

To continue the thought; if we don't know how many people work for government then we really don't know what work they are supposed to be doing or if they are doing any work at all.

Nor do we know how much they are being paid for the work we don't know they are doing, while we don't know how many are doing that work. Kayristell kalear… right?

Now do you see how vital you are and how important that 63 million of us stand with Trump? I hope so.

"The liberties of a people never were, nor ever will be secure, when the transactions of their rulers may be concealed from them."--*Patrick Henry*

The Federal government spends $10.5 billion dollars every day. Source: Tim Phillips **Townhall.com** September 2017

"When the people fear the government there is Tyranny. When the government fears the people there is Liberty." --*Thomas Jefferson*

$10.5 Billion EVERYDAY

Chapter Four

The Attack

"We must always take sides. Neutrality helps the oppressor, never the victim. Silence encourages the tormentor, never the tormented." *--Elie Wiesel*

You've probably heard the story of a handsome loyal shepherd boy from Bethlehem who got extremely ticked off when his leader, his army, and his God were being defiantly taunted and ridiculed by a big strong loud foul-mouthed giant that not only threatened to destroy their nation, but to put them all into slavery. That boy saw what was going on and incredulously asked a question of all his countrymen, who stood nearby, speechless and afraid: "Who is this uncircumcised Philistine that he should taunt the armies of the living God?"

Today we might say something like, "What the heck is going on here?! This IS Nuts! Why put up with this junk!"

Attack of Giant Progs (Progressives)

We must ask among ourselves, as we watch the president's fierce, powerful, giant army of critics and enemies: "Who are these Progressive Leftists that curse and defy our legitimate legally elected leader?" Who are these that are against strong borders, stopping drugs, stopping illegal aliens, stopping the infiltration of more terrorists, of bringing jobs back and controlling the growth and spending of our government? Who is this enemy? Aren't these the same folks that have constrained, limited and put us in this vulnerable spot to begin with? What the Heck?!

Who are they? What do they stand for? They started their immediate heavy artillery attacks in November 2016 and continue the barrage to this day.

What are they doing and why are they doing it?

Let's refer to them throughout as "Progs."

Progs are found in both political parties, but over the years, they have intensely and purposefully invaded and now occupy virtually 80 percent or more of both the Democrat party and mainstream media. It's easy to see this when you pull up the fact that only seven percent of the media is Republican and ninety-six percent of donations given by journalists go to the Democrats, proving that media people either put their money where their heart is or wherever they can get reimbursement and favored access down the line later on. Trump didn't need them, he needed us and the Progs are ticked, obviously.

Several Republicans are progressive or have progressive tendencies, usually exhibiting them at critical times such as the 2017 vote in the US Senate to replace Obamacare.

How it Works

Back in 1993, many Prog Repugs sided with Prog Dems to pass NAFTA under Bill Clinton which was repugnant. The Senate passed NAFTA 61 to 38. Of the 61 who foisted this mess on America, 34 were Republicans and 27 were Democrats. So it works from both sides of the aisle. The Progs and Repugs help each other and cover for each other at critical times, such as when they need to cast a "no" vote to fool the people back home. We can't let them get away with this tricky maneuvering anymore. We are seeing that there is not much difference between the parties, a Prog is a Prog no matter the party. A "Moderate" is simply a Prog tadpole that can grow its legs as needed to hop over the will or rights of the people and our Constitution whenever he wants to. Might be why the media love those Mods so much, too. You think?

A Fuel Stop

You can get daily or weekly updates on legislation from: govtrack.us

Govtrack.us is a great resource to use to watch both legislation and the votes of your Congressman. Later I will get into how you will become a very powerful voice alongside the president by speaking directly into the ear of your congressman. I want every one of us to soon have immense satisfaction knowing we each had a part in making America great again.

Counter Attack

We know the handsome shepherd boy from Bethlehem was David. He went on to become King David of Israel, but not without a fight or two, and not without great support from the people, and certainly not without the hand of God upon him.

What of the loud foul-mouthed giant? David quickly and surprisingly **ran toward him**; stunning him with a precisely flung smooth stone, proceeded to remove his giant head and immediately the enemy army fled. The nation had victory the people remained free and all because one tough, independent shepherd didn't like what he heard and saw going on. Read this event in 1 Samuel 17; it is encouraging and refreshing.

For the sake and future of America, it's time for some of us to hold our tongues and others of us need to step up, to rise up. The fact is clear that the President is our elected God-ordained leader for such a time as this and he stunned the Giant Progs. He ran straight toward them and they didn't expect it either.

Remember, we've been given this chance to help America, and at the end of the day, all of us who at least try, will have no regrets. Some of you braver ones will run toward the giants as a candidate. Others of us not quite so brave or talented will cover your back as your supporters. Seriously, we can do this.

No Regrets: One Who Set the Benchmark

No regrets. The phrase reminds me of a man of iron faith who also had great wealth. He laid down all he had for the honor of serving others and standing in faith for Jesus Christ.

William Borden is someone who affected the world for good. Bill started a Bible study at Yale, and one thousand of the thirteen hundred students attended it. He also founded Yale Hope Mission around 1907. Bill decided to reach out to the Muslim Kansu people in China as a missionary. He inspired countless thousands to rise up and to do great things for God's glory. He is best known for chronicling his thoughts and actions as he chose to step up with six words.

"No Reserves, No Retreat, No Regrets"

Donald Trump has been a pretty powerful guy for quite a while. He had twenty thousand or so employees, a cool jet, a couple of helicopters, limousines, chauffeurs, and a luxury suite at his Trump Tower. All these are definitely large outward displays of civilian entrepreneurial power; amazing stuff that could only happen in a free America.

He and everyone who knows him say he loves to work, loves to solve problems and build things; physical things like sky scraper buildings and garages, golf courses, pools, ice rinks, and lakes. He also loves to build organizations, not simply to support or maintain the things he's built, but to take his creative ideas and, through people that work for him, including his kids, see those ideas become a reality.

It is important for us to work together with the president for a long, long time to move the country back to winning, back to greatness, back to Godly gratitude for freedom and order. I'm thinking brotherhood and unity are needed and wanted: apply within and show it all around town.

A powerful man like Trump has powerful contacts, and now as our President, he is developing many more. However, recognize that he faces a deeply entrenched and fierce resistance from the leftist Progs of both parties and the media, all of whom live in the swamp (the swampiticians), not only the DC swamp but the global swamp as well. Just like a real swamp, it's hard to get through; it contains muck, mire, and hidden dangers.

The president and his family have literally freaked out the left, every single one of them. (them…as in media and government). Listen to them, they are triple- pickled freaked out. It's apparent as they cover up all the bizarre stuff from the Obama era by hurling javelins at an innocent man who truly wants God to bless us and wants America great again, safe again and strong again. Why are they hurling those javelins?

Answer: Because the Trumps are positioned to become the Kennedys of this generation and not the CPA tag team of Bush, Clinton, Bush and Obama. (Certified Public Aristocrats).

The left is fully aware that every successful accomplishment by the president, positively embraced by the people, will build towards a lasting conservative version of Camelot; a legacy not seen since the Kennedys, a "dynasty" so to speak, with the potential of great mass appeal and far-reaching influence by all the Trumps well into the future.

Not that the Kennedys were conservative as a family, though Jack was definitely far starboard of today's

"Progressive" Democratic Party. We don't often see conservative Dems these days; finding one would be a rare artifact indeed! Reportedly there are 18 Blue Dog Dems out of 238 who claim some degree of conservatism and say they could work with Trump. We shall see, but 18 against 220 Prog Dems are not terribly good odds. Minority status is a weakness in any democracy. An example of that is why it took the revival of the republic and the surge of President Lincoln to bring about the beginning of the end of slavery.

The Progs know that IF the people continue to support The President and that support increases, there could be other Trumps leading or influencing America for many years to come as well as multiple leaders who emulate Trump.

"What the government fears most is the day we once again stand together as Americans." *Trump*

Like their dad, the Trump family loves America, loves our Constitution, and is grateful for their lives, their opportunities, and accomplishments. Trumps hate to waste resources, hate poorly planned projects, and ill-conceived outcomes. Trumps, who like Dad, love people, are nice, naturally glamorous, and really smart.

You may ask, "How do you know he's nice?" Well, he said he is.

"I'm a nice guy. I really am. But I have a nasty habit that most career politicians don't have: I tell the truth. I'm not afraid to say exactly what I believe. I am paying my own way so I can say whatever I want. I will only do what is right for our country, which I love." – *Trump* **Crippled America**

Honestly if I didn't like him or didn't trust him I would never write this book. As much as I like him I love my country, my

God, and my family more. I believe he stands for all three and that is why I stand with the President.

Supporters not only believe he's nice, we believe he will do all that he promised to do. That's why we elected him, and it's why we will help him, because his thinking is more on the same page as ours. More Americans like the way he thinks and speaks, and are joining the movement every day. Don't be surprised when the Prog media focuses on and stirs the pot of resistance and attempts to distract or deflate the Great Again movement. They'll try to scare us, get us to run or go back to sleep but we won't. They've lost sight of what it means to be great, and certainly don't want us Middle Americans to participate or think independently. They enjoy power while Americans suffer the effects of dumb even dangerous policy.

"Strong minds discuss ideas, average minds discuss events, and weak minds discuss people." --*Socrates*

It's quite interesting to watch and study the Progs. They don't seem to see that their Prog socialist big government agenda does not and has not worked, anywhere on earth. Anywhere

"Socialism only works in two places: Heaven where they don't need it and Hell where they already have it."
--*Ronald Reagan* also *attributed to* --*Winston Churchill*

Making things "free" and promoting continual division is not sustainable or pleasant. The misled leaders of the Progs will never admit to their followers that their road leads nowhere. They aren't honest with their own people. Why? They don't care about the consequences of their policies as long as they get re-elected and have power. They forget the smaller "details" of who pays, who sacrifices, who gets hurt, what rights are lost or how it affects our future.

Prog Strategy

The Prog strategy is a combination of things the left is using against Trump to desperately blur the optics and create strange narratives. Narrative is media talk for what we little people are shown via the leftist media and told repetitively, as they inseminate news content about the president with as much negativity as possible.

You can't help but notice their slant on things by how they are always looking to impugn the motives of Trump, claiming he's doing things in concert with potential enemies, he's inexperienced, or that he only wanted the job for the prestige the office holds; as if it was a bucket list item for "The Donald." (He resisted the call for 30 years to jump in).

I have to add here that I have met many millionaires through the years and **none** of them ever took a stand publicly on anything. They are fine people but as long as they can live Large Marge, they won't risk anything since they have a lot to lose. This literally is out of fear that our government could put them through the ringer and make life miserable for them. They have a lot to lose I know. But Trump is in my opinion brave beyond most and his bravery is driven by love of country and for her people. But we knew that already, didn't we?

We often heard Trump say, **"I had to do this…I couldn't stand to see what was happening to our great country."** Neither could we, Mr. President. Neither could we.

It is almost bizarre how nothing good gets reported about the White House unless you go to **Whitehouse.gov** and get on the president's email list. Do yourself a favor; get on the president's mail list as soon as possible.

Prog media manipulation and Prog political science strategies are simple to see through. Once you learn how to recognize their tactics, you'll gain an objective position to see them exert steady conformist pressure meant to sway some folks, forming or better yet trying to deform opinion through manipulation, shedding all pretense of fairness, standards, nonpartisanship, objectivity or even truth. It's the same media tested formula they use on us to sell products and services. "Buy this burger...mmmm Juicy" repeat commercial one thousand times a month.

End of month: cha-ching burger sales triple. They've been experimenting and running their "tests" on us for decades, whittling, nibbling, chipping, chopping, brainwashing, imperceptibly, slowly, incrementally, barely noticed, clever step by step as we slip slide away into the upside down mountain of mess we all face today.

Their reporting will certainly not contain respect or even friendliness to the contaminated party. Guilty - they don't care if he is innocent. They don't own him, therefore they slam him.

When you look for it, it is both clever and simple to see them defame or deconstruct any idea or anyone they want. I call it linkaged contamination discreditation. Another way to think of it is guilt by even the slightest, teeniest inferred association.

For example: a bad dude says he did something for a good dude, even when the good dude doesn't know the bad dude, doesn't like the bad dude, and never asked the bad dude to do anything for him. The good dude is deemed guilty because of association with the bad dude. Those who promote his implied guilt seek to distract, divide, and are clever enough to know that when they throw slime against a solid wall long enough, it will stain the wall even after you remove the slime, and eventually some slime might stick to it. Case closed. Throw him to the lions. Yes, even if he is our 45th President.

Do you remember cooties? (I know this is a really adolescent example, but there are adolescent actions going on that are so baseless and ignorant that it drives many of us nuts and is solely meant to distract). But back to cooties, a girl inadvertently or on purpose touches a boy. That boy then sneaks up to touch another boy or girl to pass on the cooties. The bottom line is, when someone gets cooties they in turn give cooties to others with the slightest touch. Everyone runs from the "contaminated" ones. You're in the game, even if you don't want to play, you'll still have cooties and everyone will stay away from you, that is, until you share your Mars bars at recess.

Used against the president and his family, the cooties game is played out like this:

*Progs create their cooties narrative strategy to use linkage to contaminate and discredit all those who are associated with Trump.

*Dad is bad, has no experience, won electoral vote only but lost the popular vote, the Russians did it, bad; all bad, loose cannons; who is Jared, bad; bad man Bannon is gone but really bad now; Miller bad; Flynn bad; Sessions bad; General Kelly not so bad... yet, Kelly Ann kind of bad but don't get her mad she's a mom, yikes, Dr. Gorka is a Russian because Gorka and Gorbachev almost sound the same and both are now outside sounding bad and that's bad. And so it goes on and on and on like old vinyl records that skip, skip, skip, the narrative plays, number 9, number 9, number 9, number 9, number 9.

* Constant Media Fraud by Fraudcasters, rinse, repeat. This is meant to turn us off, get us out of the way, and keep us from getting our country moving in the right direction. (But it hain't agonna work, is it partners...as he blows the smoke from the end of his barrel... there's a new Sheriff in these here parts and he ain't interested in whatchu got to say).

*Dad's policies are bad; his cabinet picks are bad, on and on. Rinse, repeat. Bad plus bad equals bad. Blab Blab.

*Dad's supporters are bad. In fact, all of Dad's supporters are "Alt"-right fascists. The left pretty much considers anyone alt-right if they recite the Pledge of Allegiance and mean it.

* The conclusion that the MSM Progs want us to come away with from their force feeding spoon-fed adolescent pabulum nonsense is this: The President is bad with a capital B. All the Trumps are bad, all Trump supporters are bad, America is bad, cops, military and apple pie are all bad; even if apple pie smells good, it's bad because they say so. The flag is bad; good is bad and bad is good. Where could this lead if we actually bought into it? Nowhere good and nowhere man.

Our fulcrum is based on our best successes. We defeated the Nazis and slavery. It took more of us on one side of the lever to make the difference. We rose to greatness whenever we needed to; let's do it again. Rise.

It's easy to see who the MSM Progs are targeting. They have a long-term strategy: Discredit all the Trumps, try to change the election trajectory for 2020/2024 and never allow any Trump to gain credibility no matter what.

It's as if they made a vow: "Never Trump till death do us part or global warming hits." (For any Prog readers, please consider that those nations who rejected God and his ways were turned into hot deserts with famines centuries ago.) What if the real cause of global warming is blessing removal instead of too much CO_2 for the plants and trees to suck in?

The Prog goal is that we of the 63 MAGA millions are supposed to tune out, and then run silent and deep again. Are you discouraged? No! Did you buy into all the Russian influence, fascist, racists, Nazi stuff? No! They imply something negative everyday as they throw their slime. But we are on to their tactics. This slime ain't sticking. Their road leads nowhere, the quid pro blow holes who think we are yoyo's are out, their fuel rod is spent, their tank is empty and we are standing with Trump to see America win again.

The president could prevent World War Three and the narrative would be about how he put millions of Americans who work in factories with defense contracts out of work, his hair, his tax returns, his tweets or again Russia. His motive, they'd claim, would be to cover up that his youngest son Barron watches Tim Hawkins DVDs instead of the president's speeches. Tim is really funny though and a good guy too btw.

"It's discouraging to think how many people are shocked by honesty and how few by deceit." *Sir Noel Peirce Coward*

"One of the greatest advantages of the totalitarian elites was to turn any statement of fact into a question of motive." *Hannah Arendt* **political philosopher and author**

The same Prog strategy is being used on some other really great Americans.

*Washington and Jefferson fought for and founded America with bravery and brilliance.

*Both of them had slaves.

*Washington and Jefferson are bad. Everything they did for America was hypocritical, farcical malarkey, political theater chicanery rich guy wool pulling theatrics.

*Therefore, America is inherently bad, filled with racism and not the envy of the world. Well…at least since Trump became president, but don't pay any attention to that little man behind the curtain, Toto.

* Since America's foundation is "bad," and its founder's hypocrites, the Progs have convinced themselves that America needs "changed" by rejecting the founders and the foundation they laid. Yes, this is change only the gullible can believe in. This is seriously the blind leading the lied to.

The bottom line ends up being, attack the very one that led and inspired our founders: God Almighty.

"That" God of the founders, who were really just hypocrites, had to be bad - linkage contamination discredit. Guilty too is God by associating with those two slave-owning con men. Let's rip their names and all mention of God Almighty from the school text books now.

Oh, we already did that? So what now is "plan B"?

How is that working out? Seems like since we've made God small and unimportant, our problems grew so large that only a bigger government with more jails and more regulations can keep things calm... maybe... for a while. Hey, I know... we'll legalize drugs. Yeah that will keep everyone calm and happy. Perfect Prog wisdom: one nation, on drugs, unsustainable, controllable, and dangerous for all. Sheesh!

We've tossed God out, from history books, schools, law and all of public policy; in fact, they've attempted to toss God the Creator from every aspect of society, including from churches and synagogues. Oh, they might let us have "Religion," providing we agree to keep it inside the four walls, but God Almighty? Ignore Him; ignore the history and most of what America's founders accomplished. Oh, and ignore creation too. It just blew in here and started big banging out species. No miracles there.

Recognize it? Cooties and the same linkaged contamination discrediting process; a formula that usually works, at least until Trump came along and how dare he speak truth about the mess America was in! How dare he run toward Americas problems like that? He was supposed to run away, but he didn't did he?

Tweet Face Instanta to Defeat the Progs

The president's Twitter accounts: @realDonaldTrump or @POTUS

Like the head coach calling plays to his team out on the field, the president's Tweets are the signal for us to contact our reps and senators to "encourage" them to pass all of our Great Again/America First legislation. His Tweet will also remind us which politicians need to be sent back to the bleachers during election season, giving them the 18-20-22-24 HIKE!

Facebook and Instagram are two other social mediums the President uses to reach out to the nation.

"Men occasionally stumble over the truth but most of them pick themselves up and hurry off as if nothing ever happened."--*Winston Churchill*

'Some people's idea of free speech is that they are free to say what they like, but if anyone says anything back, that's an outrage. —*Winston Churchill*

"It is not enough that we do our best; sometimes we have to do what is required."-- *Winston Churchill*

"No King but King Jesus."--*Motto of the Revolutionary War*

Daniel 4:25…till thou know that the most High ruleth in the kingdom of men, and giveth it to whomsoever he will.

Chapter Five

The Machine

Progs always try to criticize America's founding. The way to combat this nonsense is not to fight and claim America was faultless, but to engage in some gentle political judo by agreeing with them in certain instances.

When it comes to the issue of Washington and Jefferson having slaves, we can't downplay it. Instead, freely admit that they are correct. While they are still in shock by us and our agreement, counter by pointing out that General Washington, Thomas Jefferson, and many others who did or did not own slaves, gave us the very means to abolish slavery at the right time in our history. It just wasn't in the 1700s. It couldn't be the 1700s. It isn't a question of Washington and Jefferson abhorring slavery or not, it was just simply not the right time to end it.

Think it Through

When we were engaged in an all-out revolutionary war, our first priority was to achieve victory, then deal with other issues. This is why we have the phrase, "he won the battle but lost the war." What we **do** know is that breaking free from Britain, then the world's mightiest superpower, and a slave nation, I must add, was a miracle in itself; creating and setting up the world's best Republic was yet another miracle.

Remember, too, that right after winning our independence from Britain, it was not until 1790 that the last state, Rhode Island, finally ratified the Constitution even though it was the first to renounce its allegiance to Britain. During these years both sides went back and forth with their concerns, but finally, after compromise by all sides, they designed and built our form of government. Our founders became the test drivers and operated the machine; a brand new untested government machine in its earliest stage. A prototype hybrid experimental vehicle, it was designed and built mostly from the memory of failures past. They installed the best equipment available to insure its successful performance down the road for the future.

If you think about it, those guys were the Neil Armstrong's, Chuck Yeager's, and Alan Sheppard's of the 1700s: all brave test pilots, scientists, engineers and soldiers. All amazing and extremely busy people, yet despite their passionate differences, they accomplished together great and amazing things, at great risk to themselves.

In the writings of Washington and Jefferson, they seemed to always be looking down the road through a blood-splattered, bullet-holed windshield of the machine, with the hope of blessing us, their posterity, with the fruit of their efforts and sacrifices. As our constitution says, **"To...secure the Blessings of Liberty to ourselves and our Posterity..."** Pretty freaking heroic, for they knew they would not live to see the full fruition of their work, just like those who plant trees under which they will never sit or pick its fruit.

The system of Constitutional government they established for us contained the DNA, the perfect genes, although recessive at conception, to eventually become the dominant gene that ended slavery in America. Praise God, due completely to the Biblical convictions of many citizens, especially those in the north, to abolish slavery under the Godly leadership of Christian President Abraham Lincoln.

In fact, hundreds of thousands of men willingly fought and died during the civil war for the principle that all men should be free and equal as Almighty God intended all mankind to be.

If our founders wanted, they could have made or allowed America to remain a slave nation, but they did not. They attempted to ban slavery in the original draft of our Declaration, but were forced to remove this provision in order to get the approval of the southern states, knowing if the revolution were to succeed the colonies would all need to be united. As a result, slavery remained, but this should not be taken as an endorsement of slavery. This is what we call pragmatism, dealing with a situation sensibly based on practical common sense as opposed to the idealistic. America's founders left slavery and our people-powered Constitutional machine as an inheritance. One was certain to conquer the other and inevitably, at the right time, slavery lost.

Over time America was designed and built to transform itself from its pragmatic-learn to crawl, learn to walk-stages, into its ideologue stage where all are created equal and endowed by their Creator. Today we are the ideologue nation, even with our problems, running a marathon for equal rights for all: one race human-devoid of color with liberty for all.

It's clear: The Progs have an agenda and they have patiently and slowly worked it on America for decades. Their goal is to undermine the heroes of our past and impugn their motives; this divides and weakens our people as it strengthens government. It denies the God of our creation and it has made us more vulnerable than ever before to enemies, both foreign and domestic. Thanks to the President we've had a reprieve; another new birth of freedom can be achieved today through us, and through our efforts. Like our founders we need to build upon the victory we now have to free us in the future from the problems and issues that we've inherited; doing so both pragmatically and idealistically.

The question today is this: Are we willing to think independently, do our own research, pray for wisdom, and stand with Trump to help make America Great Again by God's Grace? Birth is never free of pain and tears. It also requires exceptional patience. When the newborn arrives he/she requires constant care and training. Nothing is easy and freedom isn't free.

"There comes a time to join the side you're on."
--*Midge Decter*, American journalist, wife of author Norman Podhoretz

Yes, now is the time to join, and encourage others to come along with us for the ride. Get out of the bleacher seats, off of the sidelines; we are neither specks nor spectators. We are the mighty Middle, the Rulers of America, born free and staying that way.

Our side will not fight with bullets, even though we certainly could if we had to. We will not riot in public protest with clubs and masks, for unlike the Progs, we really do believe in the First Amendment.

What we will do is fuel our people-powered machine as our forefathers built it to be powered and intended for us to do. We fuel it and fight with our ideas. We debate and reason and by non-metaphysical example show empirical evidence of failures looming or success blooming.

Many supporters see, as I do, that the president has ideas that would benefit America for many decades. The Progs know that when the president's ideas are enacted, the swamp will in fact be drained and they will be severely weakened.

To prevent this from happening, they create completely false narratives like the idiotic one where they employ fascist tactics using the useful Antifa banditos, under the guise of fighting fascism. Using Orwellian doublethink, they keep trying to get some slime to stick to our builder capitalist president; a man who detests government and foreign intrusion, meaning he is the exact opposite of a fascist. Fascism is complete and total control by a dictatorial centralized autocratic (one ruler) government or as President Reagan defined it: "private ownership private enterprise but total government control and regulation."

Note: That description looks to me more like the Obama administration than Trump's. After all, they ran regulation city like the Lilliputians did when they tied down Gulliver as he slept. Fast and furious were they in their work at night, while the powerful, trusting, and vulnerable man slept.

As the swamp draining or transfer of power is going on, we, the American people, will eventually be strengthened greatly. Already, we have more confidence in a stable strong and great country; strong for us, strong for our kids, and strong for our posterity (Lord willing). This should be a big reminder to call on God's help often for America and our role as re-fuelers.

Yes, the opposition will flail and yell about their swamp. They will try to convince their minions that the big government they created is paradise. But the sludge pumps are pumping and the track hoe is digging, and I have a feeling there's going to be a lot of hidden treasure found buried underneath the swamp's green smelly water before it's all over.

"These contradictions are not accidental...they are deliberate exercises in double think." *--George Orwell*, 1984

"Pick the target, freeze it, personalize it, and polarize it."—*Saul Alinsky* Political Hero *of HRC and BHO*

This community organizing stuff won't work this time, Saul old boy. The president and his pit crew read that page from your Rules for Radicals book. They are not going to freeze or be polarized. It's called blowing the doors off and leaving you back in the dust. We are hot rod fuel and you're an old broken tool of team wreckedus leftus.

Our Great Again movement has just gotten a warm-up lap or two on the national race track. We've caught on to the Alinsky Progs and their doublethink tinkering with our machine. They are nothing more than shady auto mechanics, trying to convince you to let them work on your car, while lying about what the real problem is.

We won't let them get near it again.

Some motivations to be fuel for the machine:

"Give me a place to stand and a long enough lever and I shall move the earth." *--Archimedes*

63 million of us have a lot of leverage and we must use it.

"You are the salt of the earth.....You are the light of the world. Let your light shine before others, so that they see your good works and give glory to your Father who is in heaven." *--Christ Jesus*

The American environment is one of creativity, freedom, needs, vision, and opportunity. America is responsible for some of the most powerful advanced machines ever built, ever known to mankind. To this day, we are still the only country to ever get men to the moon and back to earth safely.

Motivated by need, Americans rapidly designed, constructed and perfected locomotives, jet aircraft, nuclear subs, dragsters, race cars, track housing, high-rises, trains, rocket ships, shuttles, gliders, tanks, aircraft carriers, tractor trailers, water jets, snow groomers, nose hair clippers, and automated factories. You name it, we did it. Or in those cases where someone from another country invented something, American ingenuity probably inspired it or made it better.

All of these amazing innovations would not have occurred as rapidly and possibly not at all, had it not been for the development, construction, and ongoing perfection of our system of a people-powered government, a government of, by, and for the People: The Machine.

The Declaration was the blueprint used to design and construct the machine of government. The U. S. Constitution is the manual for its operation and maintenance.

She powered on great for most of our history, but in recent years, someone grabbed the keys to our machine and carjacked it when we weren't looking and took off on a joyride. True, we didn't know how important or how powerful the machine was. We did take a lot of things for granted and had a monotonous, "It's always been that way" attitude. No more, we are awake and sober behind the wheel.

To be Great Again means to me that we must strive to become righteous again. Would great and decadent or great but perverse be a winning combination? Neither would great but bankrupt or great but with a deadly drug epidemic. Does great but cowardly or unskilled click with you? How about great but heartless and greedy? Does great and blessed jive with sex slavery and abort-as-needed? Is that a legacy anyone could be proud of? Let's move on and up and out from this muck.

Free, thoughtful, rich, generous, and strong are great goals of course; but we strive to first of all be righteous. This is why de Tocqueville said that, "America is great because she is good." While we at times have fallen short of that statement, at least we could try to strive towards it. A righteous nation isn't created by its government or its president. It comes about through its people. Righteousness exalts a nation, which basically means to place a nation in a high position; an opportune position, the right position to be blessed by God.

You may disagree and want only to be free, rich, and strong. But never has the U.S. or any other nation remained perpetually strong without pursuing righteousness, again "humbling ourselves" as Vice President Pence often reminds us.

"Righteousness exalts a nation, but sin is a reproach to any people." (Proverbs 14:34)

Without righteous virtues, without God-given healing and direction about how to govern, how to live, or how to treat others, society tends to fall into a state of imbalance. Disorder plus instability plus confusion = imbalance.

Those weeds again grow and choke out the good crop. We can see it all around us. You don't need a PhD to notice the decline and deterioration that has occurred just in the past 30 or 40 years. No matter how much money you have or where you live, there is an encroaching sense that something has gone terribly wrong. Things have changed and aren't as they once were. We double lock our homes, turn on our alarms, carry our concealed firearms, are wary of strangers, and trust no one.

Before Trump, when the lines were extended, as in a projection or forecast, things didn't look too good for the future. Common sense Middle Americans have long seen that big problems were coming down the pike and growing.

But let's not despair, God can "heal our land." Just get to know God again, seek Him. It's not difficult. If I do and you do and he does and she does, eventually, we the people will. I like and need reminded of the fact that I walk with won. That's not a typo. Christ had victory over death. He won. We win. We walk with won. No matter what happens to us. Spread it. Let's drive on and know that with that fuel we all win.

When we, the citizens of America, neglect having basic general knowledge or any familiarity with our great Constitution, how would we know when the politicians veer away from it? If they neglect it, would we know it? If our Constitution is neglected, we will no longer have a constitutional representative government. On paper we might, but the system only works if the people are informed and we keep our representatives accountable to ourselves and the document they are by oath sworn to support and defend (and) bear true faith and allegiance to.

If representative government is lost, our control of our government is lost. Our freedom is then in jeopardy. The people end up being limited in their liberty while the government grows in an unlimited, indefinite manner. It forces us to live under its dictates instead of us requiring it to live under ours and our constitution, that's Tyranny not Liberty.

Were we at the tipping point? Yes we were.

President Thomas Jefferson was fully aware that even he had great potential to become a corrupt member of a fierce government wolf pack if the people didn't keep him in check.

"If once the people become inattentive to the public affairs, you and I, and Congress and Assemblies, Judges and Governors, shall all become wolves. It seems to be the law of our general nature, in spite of individual exceptions." *--Thomas Jefferson*

Without the involvement of Middle Americans, ones who strive for virtue and utilize common sense, we end up with a crooked government; one that seeks opportunities to rig the system in its own favor, to enrich itself, to remain in power while they bankrupt and leave us vulnerable. I think I described the swamp again.

Seek and Hide Government

This shows how far off track the machine has gone. Consider: every one of us must provide explicit personal information to the government, and when we aren't required to provide it, they just go ahead and get it anyway. They know who we married, what our skin color is, our blood type, how many children we have, name of our firstborn, what we like to eat, where we live, work, what we own, on and on etc. Tax forms, census interrogation, (oops), questionnaires, as well as college FAFSA, banking, stock sales, and whatever else they want to get from us they can obtain from various other layered, not so obvious sources that are required to get it and give it to the government.

Government *seeks* to know everything about every American citizen, yet *hides* an enormous amount of information on things like spending our money, or other significant problems. Where in the heck do all those trillions really go? By way of quick example, Judicial Watch asked for the actual costs of the Obama's personal travel during the years they resided in our White House. This should be the type of information that anyone could easily get since it is our money and we are a government of, by, and for the people and Bo claimed to be the most transparent administration ever.Right?

After several months of stalling, Judicial Watch had to sue; they had to spend their money to get basic information on personal travel costs from this "transparent" administration. That's nuts to me, but reveals that you and I as individuals would never ever get the skinny on where our tax dollars are really going under the previous drivers. They hide everything from us and seek to know everything about us. That is, unless you are an illegal alien entrant. Supposedly illegals are "in the shadows" and the government claims to have little or no information on them. There are 11 or 24 or 40 million here but we know little about them. Right.

As I stated earlier our brilliant founders equipped our machine with the best equipment available to insure for us today its successful performance. One of the most amazing options they equipped the machine with is the Electoral College and we really need to appreciate it and know too that the left wants to destroy it.

Fill Your own Think Tank

Learn all about the E C in a great book by *Tara Ross* **entitled "The Electoral College: How the Founders Plan Saves Our Country from Mob Rule."**

Democrat Democracy - an example of Mob Rule and/or a machine running on the wrong fuel:

California regresses into a third world country by its own doing. It is also the most regulated state.

It has the highest number of poor people in it.

It has been said that people go there for the weather and the welfare. It has a $1.6 billion and climbing deficit.

It is the highest taxed state at 13.3 %.

25% of all Californians are not born in the USA.
With massive growth in its population coupled with ongoing droughts, it runs dangerously low on water. Yet its governor insists on spending $100 billion on a high-speed rail system when it could build 50 dams for water supply and hydro-electric generation. Stand Up California. For more about California see **Victorhanson.com**

Chapter Six

Mighty Middle America

Middle America is not a "class." America never was a country of "classes" where nobility and peasants were polar opposites with both sides looking at each other with disgust, hostility, and jealousy. The whole class thing is another imported foreign European piece of shizzle. It's a definition that should not be used to identify anyone or any group in America. The "class system" foisted on the people of America does nothing good for our unity; it only serves to divide us, which is exactly why some detractors use it. Yet I know it is a habit to say "class" without considering that it fillets our unity while we desperately need unity. Make America United Again.

We are a mix of people with differing unique talents. We exercise our talents daily among, for, and with each other in an amazing big screen production called American Life. There are many stars in its cast and all are created equal. Some shine brighter than others but all are equal. Some make more money but all are equal. I am not talking Marx/Engels dependent, vulnerable, classlessness. I'm talking of an American society independently strong and controlled by no one ruler, exercising our God-given talent responsibly. United Americans, free, and in control of their government together and never divided.

Class segregation divides us along predetermined fixed lines by our incomes. The derogatory assumptions that income division brings with it include: people earning less income are lazy, dumb, publicly-assisted ignorant folks who don't deserve a voice or respect. Besides what can they do for "us"?

Conversely, people earning more income than "them" don't work for it, stole or inherited it, cheat, don't deserve what they have, are heartless, selfish, deserve no respect, pay no taxes, and are never satisfied or happy. Just gross greedy people. They only think of themselves.

Both stereotypes are divisive and harmful to everyone.

Throughout this book I do not refer to or use the term "class," since it is not an American concept and I believe it stands in total opposition to our distinct American heritage of fierce unity and brotherhood - fierce Unity and Brotherhood from sea to sea.

"America America, God shed his Grace on thee. And crown thy good with brotherhood from sea to shining sea."

Let's make Brotherhood popular again; may that also be our crowning achievement. Better yet, let's work to make Brotherhood Great Again as we fuel our machine and stand with our president. We can do that.

Middle America is the largest vital part of a huge body, the core, the bulk. Together we have the most muscle, a lot of money, vast connections, the most votes, and the most influence **if** we choose to use it. Think about this, come Election Day, Bill Gates, Michael Bloomberg, Rosie O'Donnell, Soros, Oprah and all the other Progs only get one vote; meaning the poorest of us has just as much power as the richest when it comes to choosing a leader. That's amazingly cool.

We are busy people, thoughtful people, spiritual people, and basically private people; so we've been fairly silent and patient as we've waited for a leader who will lead us in a direction that makes sense to us.

"These are people who work hard but no longer have a voice. I am your voice." *--Donald Trump*

Let's add our voices together with the president and do what is right, not just what is easy.

The "WE" Statement

All Americans want to win and want to see America Great Again.

We came really close, some would say dangerously close, to losing America to deeply entrenched, questionable leftist leadership. Yet even with Trump in the Oval Office, we are not out of the woods by any stretch of the imagination; things are a mess, a deep state deep mess. A Mountain of mess.

How did we get in the woods to begin with? Was it "them" (them, as you may know, is someone we can easily blame so we don't have to blame ourselves for not doing something we should), or was it us? The short answer is both. *What?*

We

Have

Allowed

This

Silent no more: We elected Donald J. Trump President of the United States, thus beginning a long overdue revival of patriotism and common-sense involvement by Middle Americans in the operation of our own government.

We will fuel this people-powered machine called government from now on as it was intended to be by our founders. We will also pass our baton to the next generation with the idea that they too have the right and the power to participate and retain a country that is free, independent, Godly, safe, strong, and great.

We should be proud and grateful for our nation's distinct American principles and its brilliantly brave founders.

Our government is wholly owned by **us** and not to be driven by other interests.

As a Middle American, I wrote this book for other Middle Americans who want to make a difference. Those who, like me, believe this is our time.

Donald Trump defied the odds in getting elected and now defies the establishment and media oddballs who seem to hate the fact that a non-politician, non-policy wonk, non-bureaucrat, and a hands-on manager now sits behind the wheel.

Trump inspired millions of us. He listened to us and we listened to him. Together we had a dialogue about a better direction to a better destination. Not easy ones but better ones.

He reminded us that America has enjoyed better days. Trump knew that common sense had been missing for some time in Washington and definitely needed to return.

The president's goal is for the United States to be greater than ever. That can be achieved with a combination of our prayers and our involvement. These two things made for a successful combination in 1776 and remain our best option today.

In 1876, to celebrate the 100th anniversary of our Declaration of Independence, Daniel C. Roberts wrote the hymn: *God of Our Fathers*. Called a national hymn, it was composed just eleven years after the civil war. Its words march with crisp reality, hope, and gratitude. It's just as inspirational today as it was back then. Pause to read these words. Note especially verse four which is so needed for us today.

God of Our Fathers

God of **our** Fathers, whose almighty hand,

Leads forth in beauty all the starry band,

Of shining worlds, in splendor through the skies,

Our grateful songs before thy throne arise.

Thy love divine hath led **us** in the past;

In this free land by thee **our** lot is cast.

Be thou **our** ruler, guardian, guide and stay,

Thy word **our** law, thy paths **our** chosen way

From wars alarms, from deadly pestilence,

Be thy strong arm **our** ever sure defense,

Thy true religion in **our** hearts increase

Thy bounteous goodness nourish **us** in peace

Refresh thy people on their toilsome way

Lead **us** from night to never ending day;

Fill all **our** lives with love and grace divine

And glory, laud, and praise be ever thine.

I know there are some who are reading this and your mind instantly jumps to a Christian you know or knew who was truly an idiotic, judgmental, contrary, contradictory hypocrite. Please forgive them for they are not any more of an accurate portrayal of what a Christian should be than a crooked cop represents the standard for all law-enforcement. Those kinds of folks have no idea what they're doing, are immature, or are a Christian in title or heritage; not of the heart.

The reason I spend time on spiritual matters in a book about political action motivation is that in order for America to survive and thrive, America must again be on God's side.

If America is to be Great Again, we must believe that God is Great Again.

Vice President Mike Pence often quotes a powerful key passage from the Bible that our forefathers believed and contains a powerful ageless truth.

"IF my people who are called by my name humble themselves, and pray and seek my face and turn from their wicked ways, then I will hear from heaven and will forgive their sin and heal their land." (2 Chronicles 7:14)

When we read and reflect on this promise that God will hear, forgive and heal, it is vital that we notice that this promise is given only to and for his people. Not to people who aren't his, not to people who reject him, not to those who don't believe him. The question then becomes, how can we be "his people"? How can we know him?

Again, we need to diligently seek him; we do this when we humbly pray, seek him, and turn from our wicked ways.

We seek God's face, and we admit our sin, our neglect and our wickedness, both as individuals and as a nation.

Jesus Christ came to forgive the sins of every person who asks, everyone who believes, and everyone who confesses. Since Jesus was God with us, it is easy to see that this same God who heals a land can heal a heart. It's easy to see that the same God who saves a nation can save a soul. He can bless you and He can bless America. He loves to do that AND he is patient, not willing that anyone should perish but that all come to everlasting life (2 Peter 3:9).

The Bible reminds us that the way is narrow. It's not easy and few find it. Yet the invitation is wide open for all. He is patient with America and her people, indeed, very patient. Thomas Jefferson, author of the Declaration of Independence penned these words that both inspire hope and fear:

"God who gave us life gave us liberty. Can the liberties of a nation be secure when we have removed a conviction that these liberties are the gift of God? Indeed I tremble for my country when I reflect that God is Just and that his justice cannot sleep forever."—Thomas Jefferson

We must do what God told us, and then believe that since we are his people he does hear, and that he will do what he says he would do; hear, forgive and heal our land.

"Come to me, all who labor and are heavy laden, and I will give you rest." (Matthew 11:28)

"Just so, I tell you, there is joy before the angels of God over one sinner who repents." (Luke 15:7)

I suggest that if you know a person who claims to be a Christian who exhibits light, a refreshing attitude and flavor, professing "that Jesus has come in the flesh" or "confesses Jesus," ask them what church they attend then go to that church. You might hear something perfect for you at just the right time in your life. God can seek you in that way; He does it all the time. He did so with me.

Repeat: IF America is to be Great Again, we must believe God is Great Again.

The same Great God that spun the earth and positioned the sun is the same Great God that led our forefathers. Are we willing to be his people, humbly submitting to him to be healed and led by him again?

Thomas Jefferson said, "We in America don't have government by the majority. We have government by the majority who participate."

My point of quoting Mr. Jefferson here is to emphasize that those who participate always affect those who don't participate.

My paraphrase: If my people participate the way they know they should, I will do what I promised. – God (2 Chronicles 7:14)

Now you know.

Think about it.

Section II

Make America Safe Again

The Big Obvious

The information contained in this section won't be nearly as much fun as poking holes in media hyperbole (exaggerated claims not to be taken literally), or chuckling about what Maxine, Chuck, Liz and Nancy will say or step in next.

Make America Safe Again is not just a slogan; it's a major objective of the president. We all know that we aren't as safe as we once were; you know it and I know it. We've known it for a while. It's something we have long sensed deep down, can see in statistics, in the cities, and in our local towns.

Great Again or Not: The Litmus Test

I hope to convince you to move quickly by using what I will soon share with you as a primary litmus test to quickly find out if your Congressman is or is not a genuine Great Again politician - someone aware, who understands and acknowledges our national problem. If he does, will he fully support the president's solutions, which are common sense solutions? It is important to consider more than just their words. For years, we have been given mere lip service by politicians who tell us what they think we want to hear, only to do just the opposite or "modulate" until the next election cycle.

If they are not onboard, then we have not just the grounds, but the duty to dismiss, un-elect, vote them out, and elect Great Again politicians; people aligned with the President who will protect Americans. There's nothing greater than that. Nothing!

Find out where your Congressmen and Senators stand **before** primary time. I cannot emphasize this enough.

The method we'll use in chapter nine will help determine what your congressman's real position is on a host of subjects or problems we need to solve together as we stand with Trump such as: government spending, abortion, foreign aid, a stronger military, foreign aid, infrastructure, jobs, wise and discerning immigration policy, imports, drugs etc.

A Great Again politician must align with President Trump, and it is completely up to us to see that they do.

In the back of our mind, we need to be reminded that we face these problems today because people like us and our politicians have failed to do our job by kicking the can down the road. Let's solve some problems today instead of leaving them for tomorrow.

After reading the next chapter, chapter seven, you may get so angry that you will do all you can to help dismiss the entire "Let America Drift" crowd from office. I hope so. Dismiss the "Drifters" who've talked for years as things got worse, while acting as if they were innocent observers who had no part in it. Yes, many carry the D brand behind their names but several have the R brand and run with the D herd, (would that be a bipolar politician?) all Progs nonetheless.

The Left allowed us to drift into a big mess. Our machine needed an alignment; it pulled us so far left it went off the road of reason into the oncoming traffic of reality with head-on deadly consequences, very divisive ones too, not good. Thankfully, the president has his hand on the wheel and is now steering our machine towards a better destination: on the road to greatness again.

Chapter Seven

The Real War on America

Crickets

You notice them whenever it gets really quiet, usually as it's getting dark outside.

At some point, you might notice, stop to listen and say, "Hear how quiet it is? You can sure hear those crickets tonight, can't you?"

Yeah… it's so quiet you notice the crickets. It's comforting to hear them, but hearing them doesn't necessarily mean all is well.

I have noticed many crickets over the past several years. Have you noticed them too?

Smack Crickets

The crickets surrounding heroin and heroin overdose deaths really started bothering me. I heard their chirping during a series of personal events that began soon after friends attended the funeral of a fine young man in his mid-twenties.

The obituary said the young man had died suddenly and unexpectedly. My friends were told by the family it was a heroin overdose. He came from a professional and somewhat prominent family. They were in shock and totally devastated; they had no idea he was using a highly addictive drug.

Crickets

Soon after, a grieving father on LinkedIn shared a similar story of his beautiful son who had everything going for him but chose to add heroin to his life, which took his beautiful son from him. I wrote him and said I would try to do something about his tragic loss. I didn't know what or that it would involve the President of the United States. All I know is empathy is a powerful thing and Trump seems to have it too.

Crickets

I attended a church service in which our pastor said he had heard about, met, and consoled far too many families who buried children due to heroin overdoses. One family he knew lost **two** children.

With a loud voice, he added, "But in the news it's CRICKETS! What's going on around here? No one's talking about this!"

"Crickets," he said. As his words sank into my heart, I woke up to notice them everywhere, too.

What IS going on around here America? What's going on in your state? There were 52,404 opioid deaths last year in America per the CDC, which has calculated that almost 21,000 or 40% of the 52,404 deaths are attributed to the extremely addictive illegal heroin fentanyl coming through our southern borders.

Crickets

Folks, this is an attack on all of us. These yearly deaths are actual factual real statistics, and they are climbing even as you read this.

Crickets

This week 400 or more Americans died from illegal border heroin!

Crickets

To make things worse, this week 1,000 Americans died as a result of illegal heroin and pharmaceutical opioids combined.

Nearly 142 American brothers, sisters, sons, and daughters on average die... every... single... day! Almost half of them die from border heroin. Hello, wall deniers! Are you listening? This is not scientific theory here; we are talking about tangible, empirical, real-world cause and consequences.

Dying as in D E A D.

Crickets

And the same next week, affecting all ages, not just the young. This has been going on for years. MANY YEARS! Too Many.

Crickets

Not included in the stats are the numbers of suicides due to opioids, crimes, divorce, accidents, child abandonments, foreclosures, unemployment, bankruptcies, the impact on joblessness, or the costs of social services and healthcare that we all pay for.

And Sadness

How do you qualify or quantify the H U G E amounts of sadness spread across a nation as vast as America? It reminds me of radiation or carbon monoxide poisoning: both invisible but very deadly. Grief deeply harms everyone it touches and when it invades America like it has been permitted to do, it must be stopped by whatever means necessary.

Why was all of this so underreported before and until Trump came along?

Crickets

Obama asked for a billion dollars to prevent drug overdoses and for ongoing treatment programs, which didn't and will never solve nor stop the problem of these HIGHLY addictive drugs.

Crickets

Firsthand Knowledge

A local EMS fireman told me that his small township, with only ten thousand residents, is overwhelmed by illegal heroin. He told me of one man who regularly overdosed and had received Narcan a whopping 54 times over a two-year period. Stop and think about this for a moment. It means he nearly died 54 times, that's once every two weeks over a two year period!

Today, heroin is as cheap as beer or as candy, and almost as readily available.

Enter the Cricket Killer

Okay, so he's not so much a cricket "killer" as he is someone who's made and still making a huge ruckus, and making it so loudly that he has drowned out the crickets. Trumps acute awareness and empathy likewise made us acutely aware of the harm and vulnerability the left has exposed us to. The Bill Hilly, the Tacky Texan, and the Creepy Kenyan all had a hand in permitting this plague to reign over us. So, of course did a compliant Congress.

FINALLY

America elected Donald Trump, in part because he saw the sad horrible effects of the illegal drug invasion and he shared his practical plans to solve it. We've got to look at the drug crisis not simply as addiction or a disease, but as an invasion, a preventable invasion; because drug deaths are tied directly to the conscious policy decisions of our Congress, along with Barack Obama and George W. Bush, to open our borders wider than ever before.

It's easy to look up the statistics yourself and see the huge yearly increases in drug OD deaths.

Sadly, a mushroom cloud of drug deaths occurred in 2016 with a minimum average of at least 400 weekly deaths by illegal southern border drugs. We should repeat these stats often, and I hope you will too when you contact your congressman.

Think about 400 weekly p r e v e n t a b l e deaths because of open borders.

That's a big jetliner like a 747 nose-diving every week with no survivors, and as it crashes it harms untold hundreds more (their grieving families) on the ground.

Crickets

That's a busload of 57 people driving off a cliff *every single day.* Remember, these are deaths due to illegal drugs, not pharmaceutical opioids.

By the way, have you ever wondered where the opioid makers get the ingredients for their prescription drugs? They all buy them from India, Turkey, and Tasmania. Tasmania is in Australia and is the largest legal producer of opiates in the world.

Did you know that molecularly opioids and heroin are almost identical and equally as addictive?

The legal use of prescription opioids accounts for some 600 American deaths weekly. Congress, it is time to wean America off her drug problem. And we will never do that by legalizing pot. Wake up Colorado!

US open border policy was and is, at the least, every bit as nutty as giving $150 billion to Iran; a country that is coincidentally a top ten heroin producer. By the way, the majority of the world's illegal heroin is produced in Mexico, India, Turkey, Myanmar (Burma), Afghanistan, Columbia, Vietnam, Laos, Thailand, Iran, and Pakistan, with most of America's illegal heroin coming from Mexico and Columbia, according to a recent DEA National Drug Threat Assessment.

Crickets

As candidate and now as president, Trump consistently said he wants to build a wall to stop the flood of illegal drugs, thus ending or at least reducing drug deaths and the sadness that accompany them once and for all. Tell me what's wrong with that?

Negligent Sanctuaries

In 2005, there were only a handful of sanctuary cities. According to the Washington Times under Obama the number skyrocketed to 500.

Officials in cities near you or maybe in your city are shielding people who are here illegally, even though they are committing crimes, and lots of them.

While Americans are being killed, raped, kidnapped, robbed, and beaten, these elected officials continue to defend sanctuary cities. For instance, look at the crimes illegal's committed against Americans in Texas alone.

In Texas, from June 6, 2011 through February 28, 2017, 566,000 crimes were committed by 215,000 criminal aliens.

Included in the number of crimes are:

1,167 Murders!

6,098 sexual assaults!

There were 215,000 convictions in Texas, meaning many of them are now in jail, while Texans are paying for their incarceration rather than shipping them back home. Look at this from our perspective. Texans had on average 94,333 crimes committed during each year over the period of study.

That's 94,333 preventable crimes that would not have happened IF Obama and company hadn't allowed the illegal aliens in, or kept releasing them. That is NUTS.

Illegal alien entrants are committing crimes in every state. These are crimes that would not have occurred if they were not allowed to enter or stay in our country. Call your congressman. Look up the stats on your own state. These crimes are almost 100 percent preventable.

Across America, almost three million serious crimes were committed by 251,000 illegal aliens, according to the Government Accountability Office. The crimes ranged from murder and rape to larceny. The report reveals that non-citizen illegal aliens commit federal crimes at *three times the rate of US citizens. Divide these crimes between the 50 states and each state on average has 58,000 serious crimes committed by people who should not be here. Again, completely preventable!

Note: *U.S. Bureau of Statistics states ten times the rate of US citizens.

American taxpayers spend $7 billion annually to incarcerate illegal aliens; Seven Billion Dollars every year.

Arizona, Texas, and California suffer from most of this crime, but the problem is nationwide. For California, it is even worse than Texas, with twice as much crime caused by illegal aliens. Taxpayers in California pay billions a year to house, feed, and incarcerate people who are killing, raping and robbing Californians.

When will you wake up California?

But Gov. Jerry Brown, a Prog Dem, just made CA a "sanctuary state" thus the probable outcome will be even greater numbers of crimes and even more Americans will be needlessly harmed. Watch the statistics to see the results. He is nuts and delusional or third world standards sound romantic to him.

Bottom line: Again, illegal aliens are killing, kidnapping, rapin, and robbing Americans; yet NONE of these crimes would have occurred if they were not in our country to begin with. Keep in mind that the GAO stats do not include all crimes committed by illegal aliens, only the history of aliens imprisoned for their crimes. The number of additional potential crimes committed but unsolved is unknown and frightening. Call your congressman and push him to support full enforcement of all immigration and border laws.

Sanctuary city legislation must be passed, including the well-known Kate's Law, and all officials who permit the release of illegal criminals should be prosecuted and sent to jail. That would include mayors, managers, and the sheriffs of any state. We cannot allow this to go on, simply because the Democrats want to recruit more voters. This problem is worthy of emergency action.

This is a national security, community security and family security matter. Alien crimes and the drug issue are proof again that we are under attack, at war, and our own government has more or less allowed it.

But what have we heard from the left, the Democrats, the Progs, and their willing accomplices in the media?

"RACIST! TRUMP HATES IMMIGRANTS!"

Are you Progs and Repugs kidding? Racist? Really?

This racist tag is nutty, is it not? Is it not an obvious example of the Prog Repug strategy versus the Great Again Agenda? Closing their eyes and yelling "Trump is racist" is easier than admitting a big problem exists, especially when the problem was…oh yeah, allowed to happen under the watch of the professional political class. Uh Oh!

Why would Progs deny there is a problem and fight against solving it while thousands of our people continue to die needlessly?

Will

The drug invasion (epidemic/crisis) is fact and stats; it certainly isn't abstract like the global warming theory, climate change, and ice age calamity predictions based solely on a few degrees of change over the course of decades or centuries that they claim will freeze or boil all of us depending on which one is in vogue at any given moment. So Dem Progs, why not step up to solve this clearly identifiable and present problem, all you lovers of the environment and of people?

Solving it will most certainly help families and neighborhoods. It will help the police, it will lower crime rates, it will help the courts, clear the jails, and it will help lower healthcare costs and a multitude of other costs, would it not? Its common sense, isn't it?

Ironically and as comparison, only a Prog would scream that chucking the failed Obamacare cacophony could, in their scenario, "kill" thousands, even millions, all while people are really dying, not in the fiction screens of their teeny biased clouded minds, but from illegal crime/heroin every day and by the tens of thousands every year.

Theory versus reality: deny there is a problem or a real solution while treating the consequences and leaving the source of the problem alone? NUTS.

What's Wrong With Them?

At this writing, Dem Prog Swampiticians Schumer, Pelosi and company are talking (again) about blocking the budget and shutting down the government unless all money for the wall is stripped out. Are they on drugs too? We should wonder.

Trump has a simple commonsense summary: **"If we don't have borders, we don't have a country."** Nuff said.

The Federation for American Immigration Reform reports there are roughly 12.5 million illegal aliens in America. (is this the documented undocumented?) Source: **fairus.org**

Americans pay $134,900,000,000.00 each year, at a cost of $10,792 for each illegal alien. Illegal's do pay taxes of roughly two thousand a year. (Wait, illegal's pay taxes on wages employers are illegally paying them for jobs employers are not legally allowed to give? Wait again, how are they paying taxes without having social security numbers? Something doesn't add up if my un-common core math is right.)

Minus the "taxes" the cost "drops" to $115,894,000,000.00 each year; this, as we rack up a 20 Trillion-dollar debt.

Remember Congressman Russell's $85 billion in waste? He showed us that congress wastes $232,876,712.00 every day. The daily cost for illegal aliens, according to fairus.org, is a staggering $317,517,808.00 each day in federal, state, and local taxes. That is Bind Moggling. No sane words can explain this. If you put the two costs together, it comes to over 1/2 billion dollars each day. Bind Moggling times ten.

Which Side of the Wall? The Litmus Test

We can learn quickly what our Congressmen are really about by which side of the wall they stand on. Congressman and senators who are for the wall will most likely be for Trump and much or all of our Great Again Agenda; an agenda of practical common sense that is beginning to work very well already.

If your Rep is for Trump he is for you, me and our posterity. If he's with you and me, then he's for a new direction, the Great Again Agenda. He or she too hates the idea of people dying needlessly. By contacting your Representative you'll know exactly what their position is or where they stand. I will show you how easy it is in the next chapter. Not only will you enjoy doing it, you'll greatly help America and our president.

As we pour in our fuel, the machine will roar to life and move us in the direction we want it to go. With more of us pouring it in the quicker it will move too.

Let's roll to victory victorious.

At the moment, the media and other powerful establishment Prog politicians are screaming loudly in outrage, not only about the wall but about a host of other fabricated or exaggerated stories, clearly meant to distract Americans (They truly believe we are very dumb) and attempt to harm the president's credibility as well as stall the Great Again agenda. Boy, are we a threat to them or what? Yes we are, but their negligence is a deadly threat for too many innocent citizens.

Let them scream.

♫ *Scream on-Scream on-scream on-scream until we un-elect you!! And your ratings drop too.*--Sung to the tune of *Dream On*- hear that bass?

We know we need the wall, right?

Stay focused, Team 63. Don't detour, victory lane straight ahead, steady now. I know this isn't fun either, but it is critically important.

Death, drugs, crime, illegal aliens, sex slavery, terrorists from everywhere on earth...hello US Capital, is anyone there? Where have you been for the past 30 years? MAYDAY-MAYDAY

Reader, does America need a wall?

Still not convinced? Everything written here is for us to use in debate or argument to get our wall and get our Great Again President the tools he needs to finish the job.

Think this decision thru as if you lived next to the border or if your child had died from illegal drugs or your Grandpa was robbed and beaten by a desperate addict or illegal alien entrant and left crippled for life. We are all in this together because that's just how Americans roll; fierce unity and brotherhood, from sea to shining sea. We gotta watch each other's backs again.

No state is immune. Every state is affected. Don't take my word for it. Get the facts about heroin deaths in the nation and in your state. You will be shocked at what you find.

Armed with this knowledge, does it make sense to allow open borders to continue? No. As I stated, this really is a national security issue, a community security issue, and a family security issue. It's touched all of us and was virtually ignored until Donald Trump came along and shined the light of truth on this issue.

Would building a wall be worth the cost? Of course it would. What's the downside of a barrier against drugs, crime, and criminals, even terrorists? Well? What is it?

Oh, yeah, the downside. Progs will be exposed for allowing our people to be harmed, revealing their gross negligence, gross negligence or at best involuntary ignorant complicity by all-talk no-action politicians. Years of negligence, as in 400 plus weekly deaths negligent, as in crimes committed on Americans negligent, as in very little countermeasure or prevention negligent.

Here is an upside: in 20 years we could have tourism along the Great American Wall, our symbol of strength, our trophy for defeating American drug deaths and preventable crime.

Fourth Branch Power

Can We the People, the most powerful of the FOUR BRANCHES of government, by the way, remain silent and idle while a small percentage of 535 people (all of our House reps and senators combined; 435 +100) from both parties, hinder building a wall? They need to feel our energy, power, and heat big time.

Will we continue to let them sit on their hands while hundreds die weekly and many Americans continue to fall victim to thousands of illegal alien crimes, including some fifteen murders a day? Source: *U.S. Bureau of statistics 2015*

Stay Alive Stay Safe Again Defense

We need to defend both the innocent and the ignorant. If drugs aren't available then they won't be used. People won't get addicted. Simple defense, that's all our wall is. Just as locking your door at night is a simple defensive mechanism.

Just as a pause in legal immigration is a wise and simple defense mechanism, we should study our immigration situation to find out if people coming into America, *at our invitation*, are here to overthrow us and alter the American way of life. Simple defense, that's all it is.

Why do Progs scream about defense? They cleverly planned-and still do-to hijack America with amnesty for all illegal's; calculating that most aliens would vote for the open borders and open pocketbook "Progressive" Democratic Party.

Trump's awareness of and opposition to their plan stopped it for now but we need to be sure it doesn't resurrect.

Simple defense is like preventive maintenance; it is far easier to prevent a problem than it is to react to a problem. "An ounce of prevention is worth a pound of cure."

Our wall is both a much-needed reaction and a prevention of future problems, perhaps even worse problems than what we have today.

Build It Now, Congress!

Battle

Think of America's situation like this: In your mind picture a great and powerful boxer (The USA) who has a severely broken foot. It was broken when his former manager stupidly told him to run across a huge open field with his eyes shut as a training exercise, promising him it would make him a much better boxer. As you can imagine, not seeing the gopher hole, our trusting champ ended up with his foot and ankle severely injured, and a terrible painful lesson learned.

Quickly he fires the manager; his injury constantly reminding him of the manager's stupid promise.

However, he was scheduled to fight that very evening. This was no ordinary fight with an ordinary cash prize for the winner. No, this fight was for the very survival of himself and his people; this was a real-life nonfiction battle that held devastating consequences for the loser and his team.

That evening, as he enters the ring, he is suddenly confronted by not just one, but three opponents standing before him. Three against one is against the rules but they don't care. Rules are for others, not them. No one tells them what to do and no one can push them back, except the champ.

Unlike his opponents, our champion follows the rules, and despite his injury, he has the ability to easily defeat the three but the mangled foot is really throwing him off. He can't move quite as quickly. He can't spring out as many power jabs at each of them because he is distracted by the pain. Yet he must fight; his people, his family, and many others are counting on him. No one can take his place.

The three approach him carefully. Each afraid for their very lives because they know he could quickly terminate any one of them in a flash.

As the pain from the injury grows worse, he slows down some and gets weaker. This injury is draining his vitality. His enemies recognize this and know that over time they might actually be able to defeat him by simply waiting him out. The three figure, why put themselves at risk if all they need to do is wait; give it time, watch and see if he loses focus, loses strength.

Is his injury life-threatening at this point in the fight? Nope.

Will he ever be any stronger than he is right now facing the three of them? Nope, not without rest and some time to heal.

Could he be defeated by the three under normal conditions? No, never, nope, and nada.

But over time, due to the ongoing pain of his festering wound, his energy will drop; the three may gang up, get behind him, and without mercy kick his broken foot until he can no longer fight back. He may not even survive.

Can you see this champion; can you imagine this fight and see its parallel in America today?

I sure can.

What does the boxer need and what's he going to do?

First, he hires a new smart commonsense manager. His new manager immediately determines that the boxer quickly needs a cast to protect his injured foot. He knows that once his broken foot is protected, it will heal. As it heals, his optimum strength will eventually return. He then, with great intensity, can focus on the three bigger problems, return to good health and be able to cause serious harm to any one of them or all three if they try to harm him or his people in the future.

The mangled broken foot represents all the problems associated with America's open border invasion. An invasion that has drained some of our vitality, weakened our body of citizens, and made us vulnerable to enemies while wrecking our confidence in a government of progressive "managers" that stupidly allowed it all to happen.

President Trump, our newly hired manager, prescribes the cast, the wall, and for all the right reasons, to protect us and allow the US time to heal and get stronger. The wall is our protection, it is the cast that gives us time to heal and the reason we elected Trump. It's also the reason we must dump anyone from Congress who opposes it.

The sex trade is a hideous injury to the United States*. In the U.S. there are more than 150,000 sex slaves, seventy percent are females and fifty percent are children, some as young as five years old. This is going on inside our country, inside our America. Atlanta is the hub of this wickedness. Something is very wrong.

　　*This is documented in reports from the US Department of Justice.

The drugs, crimes, overdose deaths, sex trafficking, illegal entrants, all put pressure on our social services, law enforcement, finances, and justice system; draining us to the point that we someday may not be strong enough to fight back or be as good, generous, prosperous, and gentle as we could be. Remember, we may never be as strong as we are right now. So we've got to get this done *now*.

We must defend the innocent as well as the ignorant.

　　Trump boldly criticized the silence of the media. He made us aware of American border security while exposing, loud and clear, the gross negligence of the Progs.

Soon, Americans will regain confidence, feel and enjoy greater safety inside our own country, driven forward by a president who has the will to win. It is happening already and this is…as it should be!

"We're going to lose our country…because we're not facing the problems and taking action. A country that doesn't control its borders can't survive…" -- *President Trump*

"I know of no way of judging the future but by the past…Why stand we here idle?" -- *Patrick Henry*

Why stand we here idle?

Pit Crew 63 Fuel Time-All together now: "Congress build our wall now; no more dying, sad, sobbing Americans!"

Build that wall!

Build that wall!

All our lives and all our kid's lives matter!

"**What's going on and who knows what it is? Is it a Trojan horse...they don't have paperwork...no documentation...then we're bringing them into this country? Why are we doing this? We're the suckers...we don't know who they are...where they came from. We got enough problems. A pretty snake...oh take me in...she brought him in...he gave her a vicious bite...you knew damn well I was a snake, before you took me in.**"
"**Does that make sense to you?**" --*Candidate Trump* Cedar Falls, Iowa 2016

Core Issue

Trump: "**There is only one core issue in the immigration debate and that issue is: The well-being of the American people, nothing even comes close to second.**"

The President has been in office for a year now and no funding for the wall yet. Congress is stalling as America gets invaded, drugs pour in and people are dying. Why?

Chapter 8

The Call

I wrote and called my Congressman, my U.S. House Rep. He claims that the estimated cost for building the wall is 12-15 billion dollars. Based on *the price* he won't make a commitment. But he will "keep my support of the wall in mind." What does that mean?

You'll probably hear the same type of bull shizzle. "How will Congress pay for this wall?" Never mind that they blow more money than that every week (remember they spend $10 billion daily) on somewhat dubious projects that may do little except pad some department or university or foreign aid entity but little if anything for most of us.

Example: See the budget for the State Department. It's freaking huge and they employ thousands in every country on earth. You mean we can't cut 5 or 10 percent of it? Sure we can. We in the middle cut our budgets all the time, so can the State Department. I bet the President will cut it too (a 31% reduction is the rumor). Go T Rex!

The Status Quo Must Change to Status NO

Meanwhile, the death and crime stats continue to climb, and even if they were not climbing, there shouldn't be any or many crimes in the first place for they are for the most part, preventable, repeat: P.R.E.V.E.N.T.A.B.L.E.

In fact, in the time it took you to read a few pages, someone or several people have died from heroin and several Americans have been harmed; some possibly murdered by an illegal alien criminal. Sad Fact: the 2015 U. S. Bureau of Statistics reveal that 15 Americans are murdered daily in America by illegal aliens; 5,475 every year. Since September

11, 2001, there have been 82,125 murders which is ten times the rate committed by U. S. residents! Ten times!

For more info go to:
fairus.org
theremembranceproject.org
"No comment congressman?" Facts = stubborn things.

Where is your Congressman during the mayhem? Forming a committee? Studying the issue? Sitting on his or her hands? Is he asleep at the switch? Waiting for what… his recess so he can chase constituents on the donor playground?

We must wake them up, and we will! Set your alarm to clarion and stick it in his ear. We need to be his tinnitus: that constant ever-present ringing in the ear of his conscience.

Yes, it was the answer I suspected I would get from my Rep. since he is a "moderate" Republican and has been cool on Trump, not publicly supportive but far too afraid to be critical of him, a bit of a squish. You know the type, dancing down the middle of the street with that painted smile on his mask, collecting donations from both lanes going in both directions, all for the good of our district, you understand. You will be able to tell where your congressman stands by the way he responds to your questions about his support of the wall and his stance on illegal aliens; he may call them undocumented. Notice how road kill is often in the middle of the road? It is definitely not safe for running or biking in the middle of the road, so why do politicians do it?

A moderate is simply a person who is vague, a "maybe man", has his finger in the wind, goes with the flow, suspiciously on the wrong side of an issue at just the right time and never answers clearly, the mushy putty type if you follow me. Meanwhile, undefended people, our American brothers and sisters, die in the land of the free and the home of the brave. A Prog or maybe-man-moderate would be part of the "Let America Drift Again" crowd.

It's not right. Death is for eternity. Death is a serious issue; a sad thing, a bad thing, with open borders and drugs driving it right up to our doorsteps. Build the wall!

Okay Congress - Enough Study and Deliberation

What if we can prove the wall stops drugs, along with the deaths of several hundred Americans **every week?** Of course, yes, says Senator McPuffle, "Why that'd be a no brainer. If you could prove this, we would build the wall".

What if drug addiction dropped by 40% or 20% or 60% or 80% over the next few years?

We would build the wall. Then build it! If we don't build it, what then, will things improve by doing nothing? That hasn't happened so far, has it? Let's see, we have done nothing and things got worse, so that means ? extend the line…leads to..?

Needless to say, with over 1,300 miles of open border, we need a wall. It's just common sense, is it not?

Only global socialists, (many in the Judicial) who demand that American Constitutional rights be handed over to every foreigner, or some kind of population control freak, or someone getting payoffs from drug lords, would say we don't need a wall. Honestly.

Here's a thought: Solicit donations from Americans to help pay for the wall. Give donors a tax deduction just as if it was a donation to a non-profit rehabilitation center or charity hospital. It would do as much good, maybe more.

Does America really want to institutionalize drug rehab centers as a perpetual normal "industry" as common as

McDonalds with one every few miles or so? We seem to be doing the same thing with rape crisis centers with the increase in this abhorrent crime. We must affect the cause not just **treat** horrible consequences. We must not accept today's drug or sex crime plight as normal. Both are terribly wrong. The goal should be to reduce these centers because they're no longer needed. Could the flood of drugs be a factor in the rape crisis?

Goal: Keep Mexican and Columbian heroin from even getting to our people. When billions are spent on illegal drugs, where does that money end up?

The wall would also serve as protection for our border agents. Our agents would have the wall as a protective shield; criminals wouldn't know whether an agent was on the other side or not. **Build it.**

Americans are literally harmed in some way every day because of open borders and a close-minded slothful Congress, with members of both parties resisting President Trump, thereby resisting us and resisting common sense. **Build it.**

Twenty-two percent, almost a fourth of our federal prison population, are illegal immigrants. What of State and local jails?

Build the wall; it's the most obvious and simple thing to do.

War and Chemical Weapon Attacks

If we were in a war that claimed 400 casualties every week, "government" would certainly do something about it. Again if my un-common core math is correct, in the next ten weeks America will most likely have another 4,000 deaths, because of illegal drugs.

Drugs are a chemical weapons attack. We are at war and we must win the war. There are too many casualties.

In the event that an ICBM hit San Francisco with nerve gas, Congress would probably move rapidly to defend us by funding the military and demand the president attack those who launched the attack. So too, Congress should defend Americans from the heroin chemical weapons attack. Every month, American drug deaths exceed all known chemical warfare weapons deaths worldwide over the past sixteen years. From 2001 to 2016, there were a total of 1,883 deaths attributed to chemical warfare attacks over the 16 year period.

If Congress won't defend our borders and Americans continue to die at the current rate from illegal southern border heroin; in sixteen years, we will have 332,800 deaths from these chemical weapons attacks. That's like comparing an M80 to an atom bomb. Not that those 1,883 deaths are in any way insignificant, but 332,800 American deaths are unimaginably significant and many could be prevented.

Build the Wall, Congress!

The most notable exception to "crickets" has been Ann Coulter and her sobering book *"Adios America"* which is a cricket-killing, Big Ben, Seven Alarm house fire wake-up call, to put it mildly. It is time to rise up and fuel the movement to defend America from drug and illegal alien invasion, an invasion of, in her estimation, 40 million, not 11 or 17 or 24 million.

According to Attorney General Jeff Sessions, by the end of 2017, overdose deaths are projected to reach 62,000. Thus, adding 10,000 MORE deaths annually or 192 MORE deaths every week for a total projected death rate of nearly 1,200 deaths every week from illegal and pharmaceutical drug overdoses! Forty percent of 1,200 is 480 U.S. deaths from illegal southern border drugs. That's unacceptable.

Why stand we here idle?

We are Americans, we can do this. We can build a wall. A permanent solution to a problem left, regrettably, for us to solve, just like slavery. We must do this and we can do this.

Are there alternatives to that big beautiful wall; a wall with a big legal doorway?

Let's look at an alternative idea of hiring a line of agents and posting them along the southern border. What sounds like a reasonable spacing to you, how about one agent every quarter mile or every eighth? At three shifts a day, seven days a week, 24 hours a day, spaced a quarter of a mile apart, we would need 15,600 agents. For 1/8 mile spacing, it comes to 31,200 agents.

It is true that hiring multiple tens of thousands of border patrol agents would cost billions every year. Manning posts 24 hours a day, seven days a week would be a huge military-like project. Costs, over time, would always go higher with attrition and training, and all the other associated expenses that we can imagine needed to maintain tight control of over 1,300 miles of open border. The problem is that without a wall, the next Prog President and Congress that come along (if there ever is another such beast. Reminder to train our kids better so there isn't one), will reduce the staffing. Border control would once again be a problem that we leave for our posterity tomorrow, because we failed to solve it permanently today.

Just like the U.S. deficit problem or

The trade imbalance problem or

The Islamic terrorist problem or

The foreign aid funds accountability problem or

The unfunded mandate problem or

The unfunded liability (pensions) problem or

The North Korea problem or

The Middle East problem or

The education problem or

The jobs problem or

The infrastructure decline problem or

The UN entanglement problem or

The special interest lobby problem or

The drug problem or

The welfare problem or

The human trafficking problem or

The government computer hacking problem or

The growth in government problem or

The illegal alien invasion and crime problem or

The racial division problem or

The STD problem or

The abortion problem or

The "professional" establishment politician problem or

The expel-God-from-everything problem... (most likely the source of many of our other problems).

When we make God small our problems get very big. Just saying.

But just as with slavery we can and will solve them. We have the right leader at the right time and for the right reasons we can solve them. He heard the call. Do you hear your call?

Trump knew about these problems and walked out of a life with minor problems into an environment filled with major problems. Big ones, folks, big ones. You gotta admire that he was willing to take them on and not ignore them.

Okay, so just

Maybe Congress just didn't know how to solve problems and

Maybe they didn't want to solve them and

Maybe they didn't think about us or their posterity and

Maybe they felt powerless and

Maybe America hasn't had a problem-solving leader in a long time and

Maybe it's time you understand how powerful you are and

Maybe we exercise our power together by fueling the machine and

Maybe we help our President solve these problems and

Maybe it's a lesson or an example that maybe...

We should think about our posterity and who will follow us and what they're going to inherit.

Maybe we have to. We can't just stand idly by and do nothing. Hear the call?

May it be an example we set.

"If we who have freedom don't use our freedom to secure our freedom than neither our children nor our children's children will rise up and call us blessed." *Francis Schaeffer, Theologian*

The wall is a simple, easier, common-sense solution than a perpetual border force. Once built and built well, it's done, except for regularly scheduled ongoing maintenance. To find out how well walls work, ask Obama, Ryan, Zuckerberg, the Pope, and Israel. I bet they'll tell you they work just fine.

As of this writing, the president is requiring wall prototypes that incorporate solar energy collectors on the wall, which will help pay for it as well. That's a great idea and one that should make the conservationists happy, and will give them a way to better validate solar energy.

I disagree with the president on a wall that can be seen through. I heard him validate the idea by saying our border agents would know who is on the other side, which is true. However, I suggest making it of thick solid concrete so that the bad guys on the other side do not know where our agents are. But our agents will know where the bad guys are via cameras. This to me seems safer for our agents.

If someone is here as an illegal alien, somehow they can get on welfare, get medical care, housing, education, and are even allowed to obtain a drivers license. I know some will claim they cannot get welfare benefits, but their children qualify and don't tell me the parents don't benefit from this "loophole."

If illegal aliens are counted in the census, but we claim to not know how many of them there are, then how do we know the congressional reapportionment is accurate? And since they live in America illegally, we are told that they would never, oh no never ever, V O T E illegally, which is often claimed by Progs and media and repeatedly fraudcasted to us.

We simply and blindly swallow this nonsense that illegal's are just too afraid to come out of the shadows and vote to keep in power those who welcomed them, especially when voter fraud is very hard to prove under the law. To make a successful case, it has to be proven that they knew what they did was illegal. Anything short of a confession of wrongdoing means there are no consequences for illegal voting. No, never would they vote for Prog politicians who gave them what was essentially intended for Americans who had fallen on hard times.

If someone is here illegally, they are not American citizens; therefore, they have no right to vote and are *not* covered by our Constitution. Yes, we can be charitable individuals, helpful, kind, and loving, but it is illegal to enter America without *our permission*; the permission of We the People. Every illegal that votes voids an American citizen's vote. Why is that so hard to understand?

Why Would a State Not Require a Basic ID to Vote?

For a state or civil rights group or any so called civil liberty group to scream "racist" when a state requires every citizen, regardless of skin color to show an ID to vote, is simply being an accomplice in taking the vote away from honest bona-fide, legally residing Americans. Any state that does not require an ID then becomes "vulnerable" to potential massive voter fraud caused by failed leftist election policies. Why would any state risk it? Power? Was this perhaps how some were elected to begin with, (Al Frankenstein?) and they know they could not get re-elected without the illegal vote? Yet some states grant illegal aliens driver's licenses, claiming that illegal's would never use them to vote. Sure.

Again, there are anywhere from 11-24-40 million illegal aliens living in America. The government, as I said, can't say exactly how many for sure.

President George W. opened the borders then Bo erased them, and to our "surprise," after decades, we are now hearing through a fuzzy sounding radio speaker horrible statistics of crime, corruption, and trafficking - "Houston...(static).... we have a problem!" Oh, and California, Arizona, Florida, New York, but really all of America has a problem. It is a problem that in part is helping to accelerate the American bankruptcy while it harms, even kills, thousands of Americans and it must stop.

"There has to be a point to which national security trumps the idea of limitless immigration" *--Dr. Sebastian Gorka* **American military and intelligence analyst, author of Defeating Jihad.**

Complicating the Simple Machine

Have you noticed something odd about government? Call it "create a problem then create a government solution." Government is good at it too. Proven by any tax form, try to start a business or fill out your kids FAFSA. Okay, just so I don't get labeled a conspiracy theorist, let's say they "allow or overlook a problem, *then* are forced to create a government solution." For example, the Bush, Clinton, Bush, and Obama folks "allowed" our borders to be open to basically anyone, and then allowed or overlooked the fact that illegal's were able to get housing, food stamps, medical care, jobs, driver's license etc. Apparently, they of the Prog, Ivy League Left (the brilliant ones), couldn't see that allowing or overlooking all this was going to cause a really big problem or two or three. Hmmm... this sounds as if the government *did* "create" a problem.

By the way, the president wants a five-year delay before any legal immigrant and their family members can get public assistance, i.e. welfare. Let's fuel this great and commonsense idea together by writing or calling our House Rep.

Here is another approach we should take. No, I don't know if the president agrees with the idea, but we really should consider a requirement that all recipients of public assistance pass a drug test. The tests would be administered randomly per a lottery type selection and mandatory. I know we can't test everyone, but testing twenty percent a year could make a difference in other sad statistics such as crime, suicides, neighborhood violence, drug smuggling, etc. Besides, it is OUR MONEY. Don't we have the right to put conditions on those who receive it? An employer can require employees to be drug free. Why can't we ask the same of those we invest in?

Refuel Stop for the Wall - a Recommitment

We will identify any member of Congress who won't build the wall and control illegal aliens, the crimes they inflict, and the drugs they bring.

Our tactical strategy or response to their negligence is to build our own wall against any congressman that opposes this common-sense solution; a high strong wall of votes must be built to keep those congressmen from reentering our U.S. Congress. We will not be vulnerable any longer. Deport them from our Capital. Again, just like a football coach calling in signals to his team after the other side fumbles, the president is looking for us to run the ball down the field and do it powerfully.

Hear again his big play signal: 2018-20-22-24.

Hike!

Now's the time for Team 63 to get ready to knock the opposing players in congress back into the bleachers, making them once again mere spectators instead of embarrassing spectacles on the field of public policy.

Goal: Great Again and "To secure the Blessings of Liberty for ourselves and our posterity".

Hello Congress?

It is a fact Congress allows this problem to continue.

What do they care? We keep sending them back, don't we? We don't confront them about real-life problems or the fundamental changes that have occurred that they have forced on America in the last twenty to thirty years. So, in their minds they are doing what they think we want them to do over and over again because we keep sending them back, in what is essentially a vote of confidence, again in their minds.

Was it Einstein who said that the definition of insanity is doing the same thing over and over but expecting different results? This is *insane!*

Or, we continue to send the same type of people to Washington. You know, the ones who "work their way up" and are educated to be politicians; trained by other politicians to be politicians who pass the baton from incumbent to protégée, who wink wink, shuffle shuffle, know how to speak in one direction while moving policy or legislation in another direction. Call it Orwellianish doublespeakish bull shizzle…ish but you get the point. It seems to me that high office, for some people, proves to be an incubator for malfeasance, like a hatchery for sophisticated mob bosses who claim our country as their own private turf. What then are we the people in such a scenario? Ignored, comes to my mind. What comes to your?

Many get "there," then morph into slippery politicians. That shouldn't surprise us, should it? That's just who we send to represent us, isn't it? After we send them, we usually fail to stay in touch with them to see if they are doing good things or dumb things for the country.

On the flip side, they give out very limited information about what they really support or are doing as Congressmen. It is difficult to pry info out of them too. You will see this when they answer your letter or phone call, but keep prying anyway.

Your phone call or your letter represents to Congress hundreds of silent Americans. Meaning that for every one they receive from you they know that hundreds of others most likely believe the same. That is how strong and powerful each of us are. Ratio 1 to 500, some say 1,000. Sixty-three million of us at six letters a year will change the nation. It will.

"The two enemies of the People are criminals and government, so let us tie the second down with the chains of the Constitution so the second will not become the legalized version of the first." *--Thomas Jefferson*

Altered States

Trump stepped up and has changed the pattern, changed the criteria; and by his success we know that we no longer need to send the predictable, patterned, "professional" politicians to Washington. We can send the principled common-sense defenders of the people, and of our Constitution; the defenders of our God-given inalienable rights. Trump's example to us is one of a *defender*, and an aggressive one at that as he shouts the motto of America first!

Maybe I'm speaking to a principled defender right now. If that's you, what's keeping you from stepping up to the plate? America needs you. This could be your time to do what is needed. This could be your call to run for office.

We were left weak and vulnerable by our own government, due to misguided and dishonest leaders and frankly, due to our own disinterest and absence. I certainly include myself.

Absent, not interested; distracted, afraid, and too busy or a little too comfortable, where has that got us? Vulnerable. Vulnerable is not a good place to be. Vulnerable is dangerous.

We are needed, just as much as Trump is. Yes, he can do more as an individual and certainly as President, but together we can, with little bites, downsize this mammoth out of touch, candy cash factory in Washington DC, can't we?

Remember the ripple effect: our splash may make small ripples, but together we are one steady, gigantic wave, riding across the country and sweeping away misguided politicians. Surfs up, dudes, jump in with us. It will be an exciting ride.

Is America running well with its top down and a warm breeze flowing over its occupants with a scent of cherry blossom in the air? Would you agree that we've had at least eight years or more (in my opinion 28 years) of unresponsive government that has left us clinging to the cliff of bankruptcy, joblessness, and extreme vulnerability to enemies, both foreign and domestic?

We've allowed the eviction of God and lost much of His influence and protection. We permitted, and even welcomed the invasion of highly probable enemies, the toleration of horrendous crimes, the exportation of our industrial might and employment. We have ignored the mass murder of American posterity by being silent and by tolerating taxpayer funding of abortion. I know murder is a terrible word, and many of us were taught that abortion is not murder. But it is. Just like a white lie is still lying and eating a grape in the grocery store without paying for it is still theft.

Chapter Nine

Fuel the Machine

"I am with you - I will fight for you and I will win for you"--*Trump*

The President has fought for us his entire first year in office and it has been amazing to watch him win for us.

But is our Congress with us?

Is your Congressman fighting for you, or are they all talk and no action maybe men? Maybe even fighting against us.

Does your Congressman fully support our Great Again President and our agenda?

You can easily find out and you can help him or her do the right thing. Read on.

Hello, it's me...and something is definitely wrong

Who is your congressman? Call 202-225-3121 or 202-224-3121 to find out.

Or go to **house.gov/representatives**

Or **Govtrack.us**

Once you get your Reps name, ask for their Washington address and phone number, also ask for the phone number and address of their local district office. There is a local office near you. I guarantee it and you pay for it. The local office is a good place to call or visit because it is less formal than DC. It might be easier for you to build rapport with the local office staff. Your input on issues is important. The best thing to do is make your stance known by calling or writing both offices. Perhaps you didn't know congressman had local offices? Hmmm might be a case of *Crickets.*

Write your reps information here.

Your one U.S. House Representative is:

_____

Contact info: _____

Your two US Senators are:

_____

Contact info: _____

_____

I will stay in contact with them.

_____

I will no longer do nothing or say nothing.

_____

Please know that people in Congress want to hold on to their seats, the office that we gave them to occupy by voting for them so they would look out for our interests, our families, our rights, our safety, our prosperity. Do they do a good job for you? _____

I will contact the President; get on the email list in order to stay informed and be ready to help enact the Great Again agenda._____ **whitehouse.gov**

Whether you call, visit or write, always be respectful toward all elected officials, even if they are a Prog. That being said, also keep in mind that they do work for you. It's a balance thing, you know. Treat your employee well but if they're sleeping on the job...or worse...you know what you must do.

Writing a short one-page letter is the most effective way of contacting your politicians; especially when you drop it off at their local office personally. US politicians are defined as your one US House rep and your two US senators. The second most effective way is with a phone call.

Email is really easy but it doesn't get either the priority or the weighted impact of a personal letter or direct phone call. The reason is they know it is easy for anyone to generate a large number of emails and claim to be a constituent when they aren't. Congress gets zillions from everyone you can imagine every day. By the way, social media i.e. Twitter or Facebook has hardly any impact. Even though it is emotional and fun, it gets ignored by most politicians since it lacks constituent verification and private response protocol.

Joining groups who send you a printed congressional correspondence letter that you're encouraged to sign and send back with your "best" donation, telling you that they will forward your signed letter of instruction to your congressional members are mostly a feel-good type of contact. Emotionally satisfying perhaps, but honestly, it's lazy. (Note to self: People are dying, babies killed, enemies entering; we can't be lazy any longer).

Similar to Tweeting, the mass mail stuff makes us feel as if we've done some good, and perhaps we have a little; but it accomplishes very little or nothing unless the cause has a political action committee that can pound your congressman for you (pound him yourself then you'll know it got done).

I pick the phone call because it is both quick and direct. A call, however, does require organizing your thoughts beforehand, developing and following your own personal script, unless you're good at extemporaneous speaking. You can make your call either way-with a plan or off the cuff. The main thing is; try to focus on one issue at a time per call or letter.

Always remember, you are the fuel for the machine of our government by design. If you and I don't get our ideas poured in carefully, our influence gets poured on the ground to evaporate into thin air. That's what has been happening, has happened, and will continue happen if we don't call, visit them or write a letter. If they resist our president and our MAGA agenda, we must toss them out by voting against them, preferably in the primary election.

You can use your script to construct letters or use your letter as a script. Also by saving a copy of your letter or script you'll have a record to refer back to when and if you get a response. It too will remind you to confidently support and vote for them or to fiercely vote against them and for someone else at election time. We must confirm if they are doing what we want them to do or are they saying what we want to hear but not doing anything. All talk no action.

It's up to you and me to keep our reps accountable. I think **President Reagan said it best, "When you can't make them see the light, make them feel the heat."** E P H!

Calls to Congress

How to give your representative and your two senators a call:

Once you politely introduce yourself and inform the office that you are indeed a constituent (a fancy word that means you legally live in the district and you deserve to be heard), you tell them what's on your mind. In fact, your member of Congress was essentially hired by you, by district voters, not the rest of the country. As such, he or she serves at the pleasure of those voters and is paid by all district taxpayers to *represent* you and those voters. Never forget that *they represent you. If they don't hear from YOU, they won't or don't really represent YOU.* And to be fair, how can they do their job if you don't give them your input, information they need to accurately represent you and your family?

Start Your Call

After your introduction, try something like this:

"I'm calling about getting the wall built on our southern border. Does the Congressman support building a wall?"

If the answer is yes; thank the person.

"That's great, so very glad to hear it! Would you be so kind as to document my position on this issue for the Congressman to see? ......Beautiful... Thank you... I look forward to hearing more about his support very soon. Please have a great day."

Simple and easy, right? You stood with the President and potentially prevented harm to an American, possibly many Americans.

The Low Roar

If the reply you get is "No" or "umm, not sure yet" or "still looking into that issue," continue to make your point as a polite constituent.

"May I share with you some facts about what's happening due to our open borders and why a wall should be built and built quickly with taxpayer money?"

"We must stop the illegal heroin that comes into America, primarily from Mexico and Columbia."

"I'm sure you know the fact that over 20,000 Americans die every year from southern border illegal heroin."

"These deaths could be prevented by securing our southern border, as President Trump has proposed, to stop or at the least, greatly reduce the flood of heroin entering the USA."

Note: you could stop here if you want to. You've made your point, and proceed to end the call. *Thank you. Would you please document my position on this issue for the congressman to see?*

Or go on.

"Additionally, millions of crimes committed by illegal aliens on Americans must end and should never have occurred as in the case of Kate Steinle of San Francisco, whose death was preventable."

More about Kate: Negligence should infuriate us all

Kate's killer, you may remember, had been deported **5** times and had **7** felonies but he went back to San Francisco (Pelosiville) and was allowed to hide in this sanctuary city. Finally, after being stalled by Democrats for over a year, two bills for "Kate's Law" and "The No Sanctuary for Criminals Act" were finally voted out of the House and now sit in the Senate; blocked by Democrats who allowed the illegal alien invasion to occur in the first place. Pathetic!

However, and I can hardly believe it, Democrat leader Rep. Steny Hoyer, of Maryland, vowed to fight both bills by trying to get his party to unanimously vote NO on them, claiming that illegal's would lose "trust" if the bills became laws. HUH!? Americans are being killed, Steny! Many of them!

Steny is obviously a major Prog, a pinhead and needs booted from the House ASAP for putting Americans in harm's way by endorsing sanctuary cities.

These two laws will undoubtedly prevent American deaths committed by illegal aliens. We the people would legally be, or should be, afforded the "right" to sue public officials for their acts of gross negligence by not protecting and defending us from aliens here illegally, the ones they permit to remain in sanctuary cities by not enforcing the law.

Hello? Remember the pledge to support and defend the constitution against all enemies foreign and domestic? Just when exactly did that get erased from the job description of city, state, federal officials and Sheriffs? Hard to believe it, but most all officials are immune from prosecution, even as they let criminals go, allowing them to hide in their cities, jeopardizing, hurting, and killing *their own* citizens.

Freaking nuts!

"Political language is designed to make lies sound truthful and murder respectable and to give a solid appearance to pure wind." *--George Orwell*

Finally, a voice

Soon after entering the Oval Office the President quickly set up V.O.I.C.E. The Victims of Immigration Crime Office, which supports and promotes awareness of victims of crimes committed by criminal aliens. The hotline is 1-855-48-VOICE or for more information see: ice.gov/voice

Prediction: the media will enthusiastically cover VOICE with:

Crickets

Back to our call or letter, or visit:

"Does the congressman know that we spend $7 Billion every year on illegal aliens who are incarcerated in our prisons? That's astounding isn't it, $7 billion?" (Let's see. If the wall cost 15 billion and we are spending 7 billion each and every year on incarcerating illegal's… would the wall help lower prison costs?) 25% of Fed prisoners are illegal aliens.

"Illegal alien crime affects all citizens from every state in the union, not just border states."

"The fact that illegals go on our welfare system and other social safety nets paid for and meant for Americans is outrageous and must stop. Those services cost billions every year and are rising, as we run a $20 trillion debt."

"Open borders allow for terrorists to enter, human trafficking, diseases, and who knows what else to occur on our soil. Essentially putting all Americans at risk"

"THE FACTS SHOW that an open border simply isn't safe or good for America, and it's time to secure our country."

It's just common-sense folks, simple common sense.

Ending the Call

"Please ask the congressman to do all he can to fund the wall that the president wants to build; I am for it and he should be too."

Note: If you have personal adverse experiences about this or any other issues, share them with your congressman's office. For example: *"my neighbor was a good kid but she died* *of a heroin overdose" or, "my friend was robbed by an illegal alien."* Anything personal adds a lot of weight, and it should, because it is true.

You could emphasize that you want taxpayer money, your money, spent on this very important asset. While we are on the subject of money, it is better to build a wall than to pay 7 billion dollars (an amount that is climbing) every year to keep illegal alien criminals in our jails *after* they commit a crime. Once you've shared your opinion with your politician or their office staff, it's very important to tell them to:

"Please document my position on this issue for the Congressman to see. I will look for his position on the wall to change or be clarified in the near future".

Then finish by thanking them with genuine gratitude for their help etc.

You did it! You stood with Trump to defend America!

Now take a deep breath and relax.

Think for a minute about what you've just accomplished.

YOU just fueled the machine, enabling it to move closer towards building and finishing our very much needed southern border wall. And you smoked out your politician to see if they are a Great Again supporter or a Prog. You are now ready to vote against or for them in the primary or general election.

You are standing with the President.

Bask in the thought about how you've played your part, a responsible role in protecting fellow Americans from harm, from drugs, possibly even from death and all that a family would suffer from that death, **just because you took the time to do a simple phone call or letter. This IS how it works!**

It's common sense to view a secure border like we think of our own homes. Do we leave our doors open and allow just anyone to enter whenever they wish? Of course not, yet that's exactly what we have been doing and been forced to do for years; until now, until Trump, until you... fueled the machine.

You guys or gals who are tonight lying in bed reading this, decide right now to jump up in the morning, make the call, set up an appointment to visit, write the letter, and Fuel the Machine. Until then, good night sweet dreams.

Follow Up

Basking is good, but keeping your rep and senators accountable, especially in a non-election year takes a little bit of diligence. Watching your inbox for your Congressman's weekly newsletter is one way to see if they talk publicly to other constituents about important issues like our wall or budget or tax relief or healthcare or jobs or defense, or any of a host of issues and solvable problems. Some reps may tell you what you want to hear about an issue in private but publicly won't say much about it. *It's how they vote and if they sponsor or co-sponsor a bill that offers proof of their commitment.*

How your congressman votes reveals their position. His position reveals either support of our position or his opposition to our Great Again agenda. There are several sites available to check up on your Congressman and how he votes. You might be surprised by what you learn.

 Sites:
congress.freedomworks.org
conservativereview.com   **govtrack.us**
heritageaction.com   **actforamerica.org**

You will notice quickly if your Congressman is standing with you and the president or not by the way they vote. You can always call your congressman's office to ask why they voted the way they did on any bill. That's your right.

Again, always available is: **whitehouse.gov** Sign up to receive regular emails from the White House. They are titled: "Your 1600 Daily" or "West Wing Reads." With them we get a glimpse into the phenomenal energy and actions of the president and his administration.

The president's staff places legislation that the president may sign under the "Briefing Room" column at "legislation" on the website. For now, this seems to be the only way to know what legislation is part of the Make America Great Again agenda. Unless the President talks about a particular bill, there is no direct effective way for us to know what bill needs our help. I have asked the White House to send out emails, which I hope they start doing, about legislation they want us to support to MAGA.

I think they should add to the web site a column showing Great Again legislation pending-like Kate's Law "now stuck in the senate" for example, with perhaps a note to reveal who is blocking the bill from a vote. Perhaps Hope Hicks will get something like that done.

We would, in turn, then call or write our rep and senators and make them "feel the heat" and fuel the Great Again legislation. The key here is that the administration must let us, as supporters, know what to focus on. We then push our Congressmen to get it done.

Election Years

In an election year, you'll notice how quickly your call will be returned or your letter answered. Politicians don't want *anything* to cause them to lose an election. When you fuel the machine in an election year, you really will make a difference. Reps and senators will listen closely, especially when our team adds Great Again Octane to the mixture; needless to say it will move the machine.

Keep that phone number and your representative's or senator's website address. Call or write maybe once, twice, thrice a month, asking, "Hey how's progress on the wall going?"

Cruise Time

One step further: You ideally need to personally meet your member of Congress or staff members. There are several ways to go about it. The easiest way to do this is to attend the district meetings that are scheduled when Congress adjourns. Just call and ask for the dates of these home district meetings. They may be listed on your congressman's website.

District meetings are nice for getting to know your Rep, learning and asking questions; never for nasty bratty protest or disruptions. (Leave that disruptive stuff to the OFA Progs). Our best protest tool is to vote for someone else if they resist our MAGA agenda. Let the Progs keep their deserved reputation as marching, yelling, violent protest fanatics while we consistently walk softly, carrying our big vote stick towards greatness.

Call and schedule a meeting with your congressman's staff. Go and share with them that you want the congressman to fully cooperate and help implement the president's Great Again agenda. They are always nice people and they work for you.

You can plan a trip to DC when Congress is in session. You'll need to call first and schedule an appointment to visit with your rep/senator. Bring some notes with you and be prepared to spend 10 or 15 minutes at most. This is a very effective way to share your views while you look around Washington, the heart of our people-powered machine, our machine.

The Opponents

Since we are talking about fueling the movement to get the wall built, among a ton of other needed things, we should also talk a bit about the opposition, those on the other side. You know the ones, the establishment politicians who, along with their special interests, are the same jolly folks who allowed America's problems to occur and to grow gigantic in the first place. Yes them.

Don't be surprised, for example, when they and environmentalists and civil rights groups with hordes of attorneys are fighting alongside each other. Regardless of potential terrorist cells, Trojan horses, disease, horrendous crimes, or the huge costs that come with illegal entrants or the tens of thousands of heroin drug deaths, they don't want a wall. I can hear them now…

No wall. Nope.

Dumb idea, that's not who we are,

That's racist,

You can't stop drugs,

Illegals deserve to be here just as much as anyone else,

Borders are bad and so are you,

Open borders show the world how good we are.

Aye-yi-yi, isn't this nutty? Where is the common sense, the common resolve, the common concern for each other? Sheesh! Come on Progs, get a grip. We want to reach out and understand you, as family should, but where has your common sense gone?

The opposition will claim a rare bug could get squished, a wild boar won't be able to mate, a scorpion could go extinct, or similar nonsense. Erosion could begin and in 1,000 years several tectonic plates deep in the earth will move, emitting a jillion tons of carbon dioxide, causing the earth to wobble and Atlas to shrug and Mary Poppins to fall from the sky.

You watch. Mark my words. With 1,000-1,300 miles of wall to build, you can bet they will be fighting it every linear foot of the way.

Why?

Because they know we are right. They won't admit it and can't. It would collapse everything they've done so far.

When the Great Again Agenda really gets rolling down the road under the president's leadership, and with our fuel, the country will change. It will prosper; fear will subside, and God Almighty will be blessed because of our gratitude. That is a very scary hairy deal for a Prog, apparently.

We must keep fueling the machine to get the wall built, among many other important things, and built completely.

Trump: "We must face our problems and take action."

Call - Write - Follow up - Watch the voting record of your rep/senator - This is the fuel to elect or defeat them. If they won't build the wall they don't get our vote or our bucks or our word of mouth endorsement (WOM is very very important).

Fuel Stop

For a Great America, please remember to pray for the president often. Call out to God for wisdom, protection, and mercy, with a ton of gratitude to be alive in these days. These are some really cool days to be bold - fear not.

Psalm 34 "I will bless the Lord at all times; his praise shall continually be in my mouth".

"Trust in the Lord with all your heart. Do not lean on your own understanding. In all your ways acknowledge him. And he will make your path straight." Proverbs 3

"It is the duty of nations as well as of men to own their dependence upon the overruling power of God...and to recognize the *sublime truth announced in the Holy Scriptures and proved by all history, that those nations only are blest whose God is the Lord." –*Abraham Lincoln*

*Sublime is something beautiful and so excellent that it leaves us in awe and gives us unparalleled inspiration. May America be Blest Again. That is a most sublime thought indeed.

Word of mouth is an easy thing to overlook. WOM is very powerful. When you and I share or point out the benefits of the Great Again agenda and communicate with others around us the vision of our movement, we connect in a substantial way. If it's important to you that America and Americans be strengthened first, say it! Say it in church, at home, on the job, and with friends, but say it.

"If not us, who? If not now, when?"—President Ronald Wilson Reagan

Chapter Ten

What Do You See?

"Don't be afraid to see what you see"
-- President Ronald Wilson Reagan

What We See

Daniel Shayesteh was a revolutionary in Iran who helped overthrow the Shah in order to establish the army of Allah (Hezbollah) and establish the kingdom of Islam abroad. Its stated purpose: to destroy all infidels in Israel and the United States. This Iranian strategy or purpose continues today with one huge perverse twist President Obama cooked up a deal to send $150 billion dollars to Iran. The administration sent a plane load of cash, $1.7 billion dollars, as well. Why?

To a regime that has killed our troops in Iraq with Iranian supplied roadside bombs, this is a perversion. Congress has yet to prosecute Obama and his accomplices for taking non-appropriated funds, unauthorized by Congress. Like some dictator, without Constitutional authority, they sent it to a sworn enemy of the United States.

In his book "Islam: The House I Left Behind," Daniel provides America with firsthand information on what Islam intends and is doing today in America from his perspective.

"Islam is a political and military religion...every sect or group of Islam is."

"Islam and democracy are incompatible."

"The Mosque is also vital for establishing Muslims as sovereign over non-Muslims..."

"Building a Mosque in a non-Islamic society or country symbolizes Islam's claim over that society or country…"

"A Mosque is also a garrison for Muslims to prepare themselves for fighting."

"The Quran states that all lands belong to Muslims…"

"…non-Muslims will be given a choice to join Islam or be killed."

"They believe that freedom is only for Muslims…"

"(A) mullah would allow his own children to be killed for the convenience of Islamic politics."

"They are skilled in abusing the freedoms of non-Islamic countries to undermine the values of freedom."

To God's glory, Daniel became a Christian while living in Turkey and now lives in the United States. Daniel said, "The scriptures were powerfully eye opening…like a living teacher…the gospel of John was one of them."

America is into some scary stuff. Uncertainty and danger are sources of our fear, but we can't be fearful, we can't ignore what we see. We must work together as Middle Americans to support the President at this pivotal time in our history.

Eye Opening

According to Pew Research 12-20% of American Muslims believe that violence against citizens is justified. Pew estimates there are 3.3 million here as of 2015. Do the math.

Since 9/11/01 there were at least 2,000 Mosques built on American soil adding to a total of at least 3,200 mosques.These are seen as symbols of victory on land deemed as conquered.

Fuel for the Machine is the concept of basic involvement from each one of us who "see what we see." Even though what we see might be scary and perhaps depressing, we have decided, as the president did, to step up and do something about what we see.

America started as an experiment with a blend of God and man's best self-governing ideas; basically the Ten Commandments coupled with and acknowledging man's free will to make his own choices in life and the resulting consequences: good or bad, order or disorder, chaos or calm.

Today, we continue the great experiment out on the test track with our people-powered government machine, a machine essentially driven by the president with us as the fuel. Watch the daily news with its reports of crime, terror and harm being done to innocent Americans to be reminded that our involvement is important if we genuinely want to return to stability or tranquility and prosperity again. Again, we must not be afraid to "see what you see."

Together, by God's Grace, we will blend the fuel of our ideas, our voices, our hopes, and our distinct and unique American heritage into a high-performance mixture. This Middle American mixture is a source of energy powerful enough, I think, that being aligned with Trump's strong leadership is able to get us through today's problems and propel us forward into a bright tomorrow.

Are You Seeing What I'm Seeing?

For many years, I felt like someone helplessly watching from the co-pilot's seat or perhaps better said from the navigator's seat of this magnificent jumbo jet called America as it continued a long steady nosedive towards oblivion. Sure, I made comments and complained to the passengers. Sure, my family was on board. Sure, I sat near the controls sure, I knew I could or should do something, but I just wasn't sure of what to do or if what I did would matter.

Besides, what really drives this thing called America? What is the source of America's power? Can America recover? Why bother trying?

Let's think for a moment about those who went before us, who built this nation; who worked hard, bravely and brilliantly to establish it as a Christian nation where the people would rule the government with, and by their consent.

We have heard about the visionary and great Washington, Adams, Jefferson, Madison, Monroe, and the 56 who, along with John Hancock, in unified faith, signed their death sentences in a document declaring simultaneously both our Independence from Britain and our complete Dependence upon God.

Also remember those great leaders were supported by thousands of average Middle Americans who agreed with their great vision and worked with all their might to fulfill it; they prayed, worked and stood in harm's way, thus enabling America to become great. We are indebted to multitudes of unnamed heroes; ones who gave us our nation, our form of government and passed on to us the keys to the machine, along with an owner's manual describing how to run it and how to maintain it.

In grateful honor, we exalt the work of the unremembered patriots. More importantly, we commit to strive in our own way today to emulate them; each doing our part at this point in history for ourselves today and for our posterity tomorrow.

Remember that many hands make a heavy load much lighter, let's not be overwhelmed by all the weighty matters in front of us. Instead, let's just schedule a little time to protect freedom, to protect each other, to protect America, and to pass the keys on to the next generation.

If you're interested, I think we have a role together to help shape history. Most likely, we too will remain unknown, but we must consider that our efforts together could very well be vital for America, today and tomorrow, Lord willing.

"I am only one, but I am one. I cannot do everything, but I can do something. What I can do, I should do and, with the help of God, I will do." *--Edward Everett Hale*

Is it possible that you were supposed to read this book as much as I was supposed to write it?

Lifeguard

I read that President Reagan was asked what his favorite job was. It seemed to me he would have quickly said being president, but he didn't. He said "Lifeguard."

Over the course of seven summers young Ron saved 77 people from drowning. Years later, many of them were able to visit and personally thank the president at the white house for his heroic efforts.

We have several lifeguards in our family today, due in part to Reagan. We considered that learning to swim and guard other swimmers was an essential skill for our children to have; we believe that surviving in a dangerous element like water is important and has many useful applications they'd use throughout their lives.

Visualizing Reagan as a guard watching over the unpredictable Rock River in Dixon, Illinois or our vast nation for signs of danger were things we could never teach at home, or would be taught in school.

Lifeguards are prepared to quickly move at the first sign of trouble. They are trained to respond to several life-threatening situations and respond with confidence. They can make a difference.

They constantly scan and keep an eye out for anyone who exhibits behavior out of the ordinary. They make decisions all day long to respond and prevent something tragic from occurring. They stay ready, watchful and they give a lot of comfort to sun bathing spectators. They are acutely aware of what is going on around them.

Reagan's deeply instilled training and duty to aggressively, yet caringly, perform in the event of an emergency was apparent while he was president and is still a great example for us to think about today.

We too must stay alert to danger on the horizon, for anything out of the ordinary, and like Reagan, be ready to dive in and do our duty, to help our nation and our president.

Simply watching America nosedive while we sit on the beach while someone is in distress or retreating from an enemy that's trying to invade, kill our family and friends can no longer be our option.

President Trump admires General George S. Patton and seems often to do exactly what the General taught and what perhaps we should do too.

"When under attack; Advance! Artillery seldom shortens its range." *General George S. Patton*

"We are going to have it so that Americans can once again speak the magnificent words of Alexander Hamilton: Here the People Govern." *--President Trump, Youngstown 7-25-17*

Complicate the simple: See Healthcare

My 86-year old father-in-law tells of when he and Mom had their children; they paid the hospital bill out-of-pocket because they, like most folks, did not have insurance then. When their daughter was born, they incurred a hospital charge of $200 for a three day stay and a physician charge of $100. The Doctor gave them a fifty percent discount because Dad was a teacher. So my wife cost them $250 dollars. A day in a hospital cost around seventy dollars per day 50 years ago.

Today, a maternity hospital room costs $2,160 per day, the labor room $326 per hour and the recovery room $390 per hour. A normal delivery without complications costs $2,762. Source: UH Hospital system.

4 hours of labor x $326 = $1,304

2 hours recovery x $390 = $780

Doctor staff nurses fee if a normal birth = $2,762

Three-day stay $6,480. I know they try to get moms out in a day or two but for comparison I used three days.

Total cost for their daughter if born today would be: $11,326.

It's interesting to me that 1965 is when the government started really getting into healthcare. Also 1965 was the year it got more involved in immigration policy too ala Ted Kennedy.

Both issues are a mess today. Study this on your own, fill your own tank. It's also interesting to me that at some point along the way, all hospitals were required and are still required to treat any patient, regardless of the ability to pay; no one can be turned away. Remember seeing that sign in your hospital admittance area?

What about Medicaid or Medicare patients? Any emergency department personnel or local EMT can site numerous examples of misuse and abuse of our healthcare system. These are frontline professionals who love what they do but hate to see wasted efforts and stupidity.

These are the people the administration and Congressional leaders should be talking to before they write healthcare legislation. That's what is so refreshing about President Trump; he goes to the people who do the job to find out what actually occurs "on the ground." The administration talks with border patrol, police, military, air traffic controllers, victims of illegal drugs, illegal immigrant crime etc. Isn't that just good common sense?

Congress, on the other hand, relies on lobbyists.

Examples of emergency room abuse: people calling for an ambulance for a non-emergency while family members and their vehicles are at home with them - just because they can. While the EMT is stuck chauffeuring, he is not able or free to respond to a true emergency.

I have heard of many people going to the emergency department for mosquito bites, stomachaches, headaches, and a host of other very minor non-emergency maladies; because they can and it's free for them to do so. The staff knows them as ER regulars.

Let's not forget my local EMT friend and the fifty or so Narcan shots given to a local guy hooked on smuggled heroin. This guy is still hooked, and he'll stay hooked because he knows that an EMT can be called to his home and the Narcan will revive him, no matter what. Fifty something brushes with death and he still doesn't have the will to quit.

Here's a conservative concept: If heroin wasn't available would he stay addicted?

Our answer: No, of course not. In fact, he probably would never have tried it if it wasn't available.

A congressional answer: "We'll form a committee to study this and get back with you in...meanwhile here's $8 billion for more rehab centers.

Here is an idea to help stop examples of health system abuse; charge $25 bucks to every person for each Emergency Room visit. If the person doesn't have it at the time, simply withdraw $25 bucks from the person's public assistance account. That's what happens to a taxpayer when they pay a co-pay. The money is no longer available for food or to pay other bills, but they do receive medical care. Medical care is a good thing and contributing a little toward the benefit of receiving it would keep it from being abused. Everyone gets care while everyone pays a little.

Where is Captain Common Sense? Up, Up and...Delay

So, let's think this through from a commonsense point of view.

If anyone can get treated at any hospital for free, what happens to costs? They go up.

If people have a habit of using emergency rooms because it's free to them, even when their issue is not an emergency, what happens to costs? They go up.

What happens when our borders are opened and millions of illegal aliens use the aforementioned available services? Costs go up.

What happens when millions of legal immigrants go on public assistance and use the same available services? Costs go way up. But they can and will most likely vote for Progs. Hmmm.

What happened when our government "negotiated" NAFTA and lost millions of American jobs? Families had to go on public assistance; and the costs...? They went up.

With open borders and the massive influx of heroin from Mexico and Columbia, which caused it to become cheaper than beer or candy, what has happened?

Crime, healthcare, law enforcement, and prison costs all went up. We must never forget that funerals, burial plots, and casket sales are on the rise due to our government's negligent policies. Crickets and Caskets is not a Broadway musical, but a sellout none the less. A sellout of silence, that is until Trump.

Conspiracy or Stupidity; a Bigly Fuel Stop

Do we have these problems due to sheer ignorance, or are they allowed to happen or crafted to happen? Are they intended to bring about bigger government and potentially bankrupt us? Remember the "Cloward-Piven strategy" from chapter one?

Is it simply gross negligence on the part of our elected officials as a whole? Are they really that stupid and lacking of common sense or skill and vision?

Is America being systematically attacked with an objective to weaken us and the resolve of our people so that Socialism, Communism, or Islam can more easily conquer us?

Our steering wheel was in the hands of leftists for so long they steered us right smack into a storm. The president is now in the driver's seat. The president is the new direction and God has placed him in the position to lead us through this storm. All storms pass and this one will as well.

It is exciting to consider we are now moving in a direction of greatness, goodness, and confident strength. Not only can I do all things through Christ who strengthens me, but you too can do all things and so can America.

Back to Create and Complicate

Hmmm, so it appears that giving something away, calling it a right, and allowing non-citizens to use it costs Americans a lot of money. That's OPM, Other People's Money. What have we the people gotten as a return on our investment?

Speaking of money; that dollar my father-in-law spent in 1965 is equivalent to around eight dollars today. Therefore, the cost of my wife's birth today, using only inflation adjusted dollars, would be $2,400.00, definitely nowhere near the $11,326.00 that insured patients see today.

Granted that today, there are differences that won't allow us to compare apples to apples exactly because we have costs associated due to amazing advances in medical technology and methods, which definitely add value and cost.

Let's also not forget that doctors are often sued and the cost of malpractice insurance is expensive, with premiums costing some doctors almost three thousand dollars a month.

With these differences in mind, for arguments sake, let's generously triple the cost of her birth to $7,000.00. At seven grand, our costs are now heavily adjusted for inflation, for epidurals, pre-birth monitoring, Ultrasounds, advanced technology and advanced nursing/physician care procedures and facilities. Don't forget the ever present hovering pressure of compliance with government regulations and paperwork requirements, huge malpractice insurance policies and lest we forget, today's doctor has lost all authority to provide a discount to anyone, probably from fear of being accused of discrimination. So a $2,400 bill may justifiably become $7,000 in light of our time-tunnel scenario and the realities we have today.

Where Does the Dough Go?

In our simple example, the obvious question is: where does the remaining $4,326 go?

How can we convert so generously from $300 to $7,000 and still see so much of a difference? On the surface it seems that we are all paying for the abuses in the system. American taxpayers and those who actually pay healthcare premiums, either employees or employers or a combo of both, are paying for free care for many and for the abuses of others. Americans provide free care for illegal aliens and anyone else who can't or doesn't have the ability to pay. By the way, were millions of illegal aliens ever calculated into the load placed on our nation's healthcare system? I doubt it. Was the influx of 72 million legal immigrants every figured in either? I doubt it, probably just an oversight, right?

Doesn't this basic example remind you of the attitude of Progs? I can almost hear it: "Just do it and let someone else deal with it later." Do you hear it too? The old kick the can down the road for someone else to pick up later deal. The outcome of their policies: you've heard it before...a mess.

The president is dealing with their messes. He's picked up the can to either crush it and reuse it, or toss it into the dump of useless waste. Let's do our part to help him by staying informed and keeping our reps accountable.

Lastly how much do healthcare insurance companies make? Just as importantly, how much does our own government consume or suck up during the process? Why is it that before the government got involved in healthcare a baby delivery cost $300 and now costs $11,326 but should cost around $7,000 at the most? By the way immigration in 1965 was 1/5 of what it is today and the stats for abortion…zero.

It seems our $4,326 overcharge represents free stuff given out to… who knows who. We don't know, do we? To quote that great "philosopher" Gen. Anthony McAuliffe who at the Battle of Bastogne told the Germans who demanded surrender: **"Nuts!"**

Why is government involved in healthcare at all, and what does it do? Shuffle paper and give out free stuff all the while paying billions to insurance company "pals" who donate across the street from our Capital, hosting re-election "receptions" for members of Congress.

The fact is, it didn't run its own taxpayer funded Veteran hospitals very well, so why are its hands anywhere near the private hospitals?

Think about how poorly they treated our veterans; it's shameful and these amazing people fought in the Middle East, Vietnam, South Korea, Germany, and the Pacific. Our heroes were abused, neglected and made vulnerable by the government and a system that they fought to protect. Unreal. But again, it was only Trump who spoke up loudly and in anger about the neglect.

The DOJ often announces that it finds fraud, so yes, as with anything involving massive amounts of money, healthcare fraud must account for a significant portion of our $4,326 mystery.

Healthcare, immigration and growth in government all have a common thread: Allow a problem to occur, then create a complicated and costly government solution. The solution seems to always end up costing more than projected, and seems to grow and strengthen the government while providing less and leaving us of the Mighty Middle dependent and vulnerable.

Until Trump stepped up, many of us heard very little about the problems our politicians had created or allowed to happen, forgot to consider or just overlooked or didn't see coming. All are supposedly honest mistakes, just accident, just oversights. Again crickets and I say again, bull shizzle. Nuts.

Or as Trump called them, "really stupid decisions made by stupid people who don't know what the hell they're doing."

Stupid is stupid, and we can all call our elected official, our U.S. Rep, and discuss with them what is important to us.

Have you noticed that many of the same folks who allowed these problems to fester use this line on us: "I am asking for your vote. Please reelect me; I'm the experienced candidate. I'll do much better for you tomorrow. I promise."

Remember the 18-20-22-24 hike? Boot Em! See a Great Again site: **magacoalition.com**

Each Congressman gets paid $174,000 per year, plus benefits. In some years, such as 2012, congress had 239 days off which included the entire month of August. Do the math.

They also have a $900,000 staff allowance and a $250,000 office and travel expense budget, not to mention free airport parking, free gym, and a retirement plan that is many times better than ours.

They deserve everything they get, and compared to the private sector, the pay is comparable to what the average corporate attorney or a vice-president gets. Associate Attorneys get from $160-204,000 annually to start. General Counselors get an average of $656,000. My point here is to remind us that we pay our Congressman fairly. They work for us and are there in DC to represent our interests, our values, our pocketbooks, our safety, and our future hopes as they defend and support our Constitution.

We just need to be sure they *do the job we are paying them to do.* We supply the Fuel and they are paid to insure domestic tranquility, establish justice, defend u, and secure the blessings of liberty for us and the next generations. Doing so was once known as following or abiding by the Constitution. If they won't, we fire them and hire people who will. And it's such a quick thing to do. Every two years we have the opportunity to make a change. Six years for senators. That's called term limits - under our terms. We the people limit and govern the government by our votes; knowing who we vote for and if they are a Great Again statesman will MAGA. It's not all that hard folks we can do this. Believe me.

See that it's Step up Time

We are the working, praying, serious forward-thinking, family-building, fun-loving, inquiring, teachable, patriotic ambitious, comfortable, repentant, seekers, sinners, learners, minions, managers, unionists, antiracist, beginners, nationalists and labelers.

We have been labeled thinkers, doers, drinkers, sober, squeakers, seniors, goers, mowers, doubters, lowers, movers, gorgeous middles, lovely uppers, handsome mentioned, mansioned, timid generalist, balloonist cartoonist, calloused optimists, leakers, hopefuls, bathers, sprinklers, rowers, poolers, sneakers, pullers, richer, poorer, have, have not's, visionary, myopic, junior specialist, prudent students, muscles, and crooners. Who sense it's time to step up to do what we've never done before.

Step up, *do something great today for posterity tomorrow,* and leave a legacy that can affect our national direction from that of sputtering, stalled, fearful and uncertainty, back to one of confident greatness; one that is God honoring, filled with life, peace, grace, and joy.

Yes, Americans are different, but together we are powerful, we are: Fuel for the Machine.

Our ideas contain both experience and vision. Vision looks ahead and down the road at the consequences, either good ones or bad. Trajectory matters. See where we land, see ahead.

Shall we descend or ascend?

Rise or fall or continue to stall?

Slide or ride or be a guide for posterity to see?

Rejoice in justice or allow injustice to go unchallenged?

Hope or fear?

What are your ideas, your vision? They might make a huge difference, whatever they are. Stand with us.

If my labels did not describe you, then who are you and what is your legacy?

Describe yourself at the moment - write it here

_____

Legacy time: See and describe who you want to be known as

_____

Chapter Eleven

The Party

Has anyone noticed that even with an abundance of Ivy League leaders in charge (our four former Harvard and Yale educated Presidents not withstanding), we now have more enemies, long wars, more illegal drugs, more crimes, more deficit spending, greater national debt, more division, more poverty, and a less accountable government?

Smart people or what? Yes, they are smart and they knew their actions would never or hardly ever affect their own lives. Some were smart enough to time delay their policy bombs to hit after they left office with most of them being non-sustainable such as open borders or escalating healthcare costs or deficits and war. NAFTA was a bomb first assembled by Geo H. W. Bush with its fuse lit by Bill Clinton. The blast effects are still felt today until Trump kicked the bomb back into the tent of those who made it. The same happened with Bo and the Obamacare fused bomb and the Iranian fused bomb. Both assembled with Democrat "brilliance" aided, abetted, and lit with help from a few compliant, weak Republicans. Talk about collusion… sheesh!

A Dangerous Man with Very Dangerous Beliefs

Before we get too far away from thoughts about America's primary elections as it relates to the presidency and choosing our driver, may I ask you a question?

Did it strike you as odd that one of the "leading" candidates was an avowed "democratic socialist?"

Trotted out by the media as if his socialism was "no big deal," even though he was not a Democrat, but in the Senate he "caucused" with them; Bernie was the only avowed socialist to serve in the US House.

In 2007, Vermont sent Bernard Sanders to the US Senate. Often, he is called an "Independent" by the media but Bernie calls himself a democratic socialist and claims everyone in Vermont knows him to be a socialist. Study him and his policies for yourself, but his plan to raise the capital gains tax from 20% to 64.2% (what's the point 2 for?) reveals a mind that forcibly takes from some and gives it to others. This duplicity always starts with the big easy targets. Eventually those run dry and the smallest producers (you and I) become the targets. Think Venezuela - not good.

I know many think: how can a guy that looks and sounds like Grandpa Simpson be dangerous? Answer: He has dangerous ideas which would further erode our freedom, change our Republic, and move us towards something we as individuals would be powerless to stop. Gradually, soft-sounding socialism forces everyone to give up what they've earned for the "greater good." Its takes away incentives since hard work and innovation are not rewarded. The few that have power, using bigger but empty promises, get more power over others who are totally dependent on the state. Unsustainable-vulnerable-stupid and if we allow ourselves to be pushed further into the river of soft socialism it will gradually turn into an inescapable current dragging our posterity over the falls to ruin. We hear the raging danger ahead. Do we stay in the stream or rush back to the banks of our independent people-powered republic? It is up to us.

"Socialists like to get people dependent on the state. You never build a great society that way. Socialists don't like people to choose for themselves for they might not chose socialism. The problem with socialism is that you

eventually run out of other people's money."—*Margaret Thatcher* compilation

America has had two historical occurrences where third parties made it even remotely near actual presidential consideration. One was Reform Party founder Ross Perot, who ran as an independent in 1992. He garnered almost 19% of the vote by rightly claiming that NAFTA would suck millions of jobs from America. President George H. W. Bush was all for international trade deals and had signed the bipartisan GATT agreement. The Democrat opponent was an obscure young Governor from Arkansas by the name of William J. Clinton. Because of Perot's strong stand on trade, he divided the ticket and Clinton defeated Bush, won the Presidency and enjoyed and got credit for the economic legacy created by Ronald Reagan. Ironically, Clinton signed NAFTA, which we now know transferred millions of our jobs, plus innovation and technology overseas, effectively crippling America for decades. That is, until now.

Another third-party experience, actually four parties if you include the socialist Eugene Debs, was in 1912. It too had very mixed results, with consequences that continue to affect America to this very hour. After Republican President Teddy Roosevelt left office, he was not at all happy with his predecessor, William Howard Taft. Roosevelt decided to run against Taft in the Republican primary and lost. After his loss, he formed the left leaning Progressive party, also dubbed the Bull Moose Party by the press.

The once popular former president ended up doing exactly what Ross Perot did, garnering 27% of the vote and the election went to an obscure former college president who had served two years as the Democratic governor of New Jersey by the name of Woodrow Wilson. Under Wilson, the Federal income tax was imposed, tariffs on imports were reduced, and the Federal Reserve was established. Look up what else Wilson did for us.

I share this brief history to remind us that, while we need to fight against the establishment and try to drain the swamp, we need to do so wisely by being wary of and sensitive to the danger that three or more political parties can have in a presidential race or in any election. In each case, it only served to help the Progs, never the freedom-loving constitutionalist candidate, sending America in unexpected directions as well as diluting the power of our votes.

Imagine what would happen if we were to have a repeat of the elections mentioned above and an avowed socialist was elected. With the precarious state our country is in today, there are no guarantees next time. We certainly can prevent that possibility from ever occurring by closely studying the candidates and voting en masse in every primary; "nip it in the bud," as the other Barney (Fife not Frank) used to remind us.

Sadly, the once mighty Democratic Party, the party of Thomas Jefferson and Andrew Jackson (who had the privilege of being president during the only time the nation had no debt) looks to have fully embraced socialism, choosing to instead call it "progressive." They've taken over America's healthcare system, which amounted to a takeover of 1/6 of the US economy and led America into 20 trillion dollars of debt. Of course, all this occurred because limp-wristed Repubs lacking true grit sipped their martinis and watched.

Teddy's colorful Bull Moose foray into the progressive forest was the first of two damaging examples. Today's obstructionist Progs and their Bull Shoot party of empty promises could have cost us our country if Trump hadn't won.

While many democracies have multiple political parties, in America with its representative republic government, the two-party system has proven consistently to work the best. The main reason is we enjoy focused efficiency; two are simply efficient and it is much easier to focus on two parties rather than multiple parties. Yes, a spirited primary with multiple candidates within both parties is really good and has proven to be the best way to reflect our will of who goes on to the general election.

If you aren't happy with one of the two parties, get involved and work to change the party. Anyone wanting to start a new party ends up diluting votes and shaving the margins down from one or both party candidates. I recommend staying away from all third parties, libertarian, Green, Socialist, Constitution, or any other. They always lose and as intended siphon votes from the incumbent. Kasich, if he doesn't become a Democrat beforehand, will probably be a third-party candidate in 2020.

Europe today is a mess in part, I believe, due to multiple party systems. France has six main political parties and has changed its government nine times since 1789 with its newest constitution written in 1958. France has 908 Legislators compared to 535 in America. This is especially noteworthy when you consider how much bigger we are than France.

Italy has the distinction of changing its government sixty-four times in just the last seventy years! As an example of a mess, in 2013 Italy had one hundred sixty-nine - that's 169! - political parties, movements, and groups on the ballot for voters to sift through.

Italy's predicament looks like a large scale "divide and conquer" strategy, a massive dilution of not only votes but the will and hopes of the people. With so many issues, very few voters have the time and ability to sift through and confidently understand each clearly enough to make an informed decision.

Could you? I certainly could not. Look over a restaurant menu with twenty-five choices and you'll see what I'm going for here.

Do you think there is a correlation in those countries between multiple parties and their instabilities? Oh, I should have had the fish but I went for the Fennec Fox because it sounded so different.

America should continue to keep things simple with two parties. This necessitates that we of the middle stay involved. The more involved we are the less manipulated and cheated we will be. And we can shape and modify things and be involved much easier with only two parties. After all, aren't Americans known for simple efficiency, streamlining, getting to the point, pounding it out, and getting on with it? Well we were, and we can certainly be again. Today, plan to call your local party leader and attend a meeting. You'll be surprised at how welcomed you'll be. Tell them Trump sent you.

Trump Identified Problems

Remember that unexpectedly and with great ridicule from the establishment, Trump stepped up and into the primary arena with his head held high, little to gain, and much to lose. He quickly and accurately ridiculed many of the other candidates as being little more than all-talk do-nothing politicians.

With his distinct differences, valor, and bravado, along with boldness, humor and candor, he reminded us that we are all in this together and we couldn't let "them" get away with harming our great big beautiful country any longer. We couldn't allow "them" to continue to cripple America, our neighbors, our allies, and our friends any longer.

**"It's time to bring America back to its rightful owners-
the American people. I'm not going to play the same game
politicians have been playing for decades-all talk no action,
while special interests and lobbyists dictate our laws. I am
shaking up the establishment on both sides of the political
aisle because I can't be bought. I want to bring America
back, to make it great and prosperous again, and to be sure
we are respected by our allies and feared by our
adversaries."** *--Donald Trump,* **Crippled America**

Progressives reside in both parties, their objective was, is,
and will continue to be to limit us of the big and bold, brave
and beautiful, American middle. To remove from us and
especially from our children, most standards of comparison, to
control us, to contain, to numb, and even bore as many of us as
possible during future elections. And that goes double for
future primaries. They want us and our children to simply give
up, throw up, and stop participating in elections or making any
further attempts to be fuel for the machine. (Hear them: You
don't matter, you're only one person, and who do you think
you are anyway? Stay home). I've heard so many people claim
to be "sick" of our elections proving that the monotonous,
parroting, crisis-driven hysteria sound bite narratives blasted
and puked out on us from the left in media **do in fact work**.
They move many Americans away from active study and
involvement during our colorful and robust election process.
Let's be sure to not let that happen to us as we propel down the
track. We are smarter than they think. Always remember that.

The Major Shakers and Movers = US

**"We in America don't have government by the
majority. We have government by the majority who
participate."** *--Thomas Jefferson,* **Author of the Declaration
of Independence**

Our election procedure has worked quite well for over two
hundred years. We should always remember that this process,

no matter how loud or hot or volatile or mean-spirited it seems to get, this process is a really wise alternative to… shooting bullets at each other. Our elections take the place of a coup or civil war. The best way to change direction is with a mighty debate, a war of clear ideas beginning before and during our primaries. Elections are privileges. A primary and the general election are essentially mini-wars. In fact, a campaign is defined as "a series of military operations intended to achieve a particular objective, confined to a particular area, or involving a specified type of fighting." That means outcomes and consequences for everyone, whether they are involved or not.

In America, our elections are opportunities to overthrow any and all government officials. Yep, git em out of office whenever we the people think it's necessary to give em the boot.

My unrefined definition of a campaign: "A fight that involves people with ideas who are fighting against other people who hold different ideas. However, the outcome of that fight is decided by yet other people who are not in the fight directly but who will be most affected by the ideas of those doing the fighting." Trump was the only one truly fighting, while the other candidate was pre-coronated by media and establishment Progs, hoping she would say and do little to reveal her true intentions to finish carrying out the so-called Fun Duh Mental Transformation of America by Bo.

We will be affected. We must vote. We must fight. Trump won because we liked his ideas and we liked the way he fought. He fought for us. He fights for America today.

Oh yes, that reminds me, let's right now give a big shout-out to those I now view as the flim flam, pro quid pro blowhole, Ivy league legal eagle political get-alongs who *allowed* America to become both a bankrupt and vulnerable nation. The swamp, its creatures and its feeders, are real. We must again thank President Trump for making us aware of the swamp; but it's going to take all of us pushing our representatives and senators to drain it. More than likely, we will need to quickly and efficiently toss from office and replace all representatives and all senators who resist draining the swamp in 2018 and 2020. Yes, even those politicians with familiar names. We can and we must! The primaries are the best moment to strike.

Remember that far **fewer people participate in the primaries, thus magnifying your influence.** You and I can make a huge difference by clipping the wings of the strongest vulture first, thereby giving space for a new eagle; a Great Again Eagle, to soar.

Most of us know this isn't a very good situation for America to be in. It has taken decades to end up where we are now. Incrementally, little by little, we have declined and it will take slow and steady effort from all of us to return America to Greatness, but by God's grace we've been given a reprieve and a pivotal one at that.

After clearing the great hurdle of the primary campaign and gaining an opponent in the general election, a continuation of the idea debate war moves forward with even greater force and momentum. The general election "war campaign" has many battle strategies, one being the rallying of all troops, perhaps even getting some troops from the other side to break rank.

Spending money wisely, especially when it's mostly your own, and spending your time wisely in states where it could make a calculated difference is a vital strategy that could make the difference between victory and defeat.

Case in point: Harpersfield Township, Ohio was a brilliant move by Trump which pulled votes from both Ohio and Pennsylvania. Not only was the world-famous Spire Institute packed to maximum capacity, nearly 10,000 people had to be turned away. Right Side Broadcasting Network showed that an additional 220,030 viewers watched the October 27th rally online. Not having a Presidential visit since the days of JFK, Trump won both states in a landslide. Ohio was a landslide victory of almost 10% and Pennsylvanian counties went Trump 56 to 11.

Trump's 10% victory in Ohio was especially poignant considering the pathetic attitude and actions of Ohio Governor John Kasich who snubbed and blunted Trump every chance he could up & through November 8th. Even today, Kasich continues to campaign, though no one knows why or what for, giving bland and predictable establishment speeches.
No agenda there, huh?

An Ohio Detour

While I'm on John Kasich, Ohio's two-term whiner turned out to be a big bold-faced two-timer when he vetoed Ohio's prolife Heartbeat bill. He choked. He folded just when he could have stood out and led with light; instead he dropped back into the shallow cave of moderate compromise. His veto reason: he was afraid of the bill's legal challenges and that SCOTUS would overturn it.

But **maybe** it would have stood.

The big question since 1973 has always been "when does life begin?" SCOTUS will not rule on this issue until they have a case to consider. Why not make the Ohio Heartbeat bill the one they heard? That could have been the greatest debate of the decade with support from medical technology and science.

Roe v. Wade left the door open for that question to be answered, stating that when the question - when does life begin? - is answered, either the ruling would be modified or abolished.

Ironically, some robot on Mars (so researcher's claim, as they file yet another million-dollar grant request) "discovers" two moldy bacteria cells or a water crystal under a rock. The discovery has everyone excited! Life on Mars! What life no one knows, but "Life" nevertheless. So our country is solidly Prolife... on Mars. Let that slosh around your think tank.

But the serious profound question of when does life begin isn't answered with living human cell evidence found in abundance here on earth, that's not acceptable to the court. The question can be clearly and honestly answered by the heart. The heart has tons of evidence for us to explore, without robots or tax dollars.

The spark of life begins with the heartbeat three weeks after conception. Life continues until the heart stops. (If you're 30 your heart has been beating for 30 years and 8 months). Life ends when the heart beat stops. If Life ends when the heart stops beating, this proves logically and scientifically that life begins when the heart starts beating. Why then aren't we a nation for life? What are we waiting for? Until the child can tell us he or she is alive? They scream in pain while in the womb, that we already know.

Illness or old age doesn't kill us until our heart stops. Ohio had a chance to show common sense about life, a reasonable and simple diagnosis with nothing gray or questionable. A true black and white, crystal clear issue summed up like this: if the baby's heart is beating that baby is alive. Let's pass a national heartbeat bill and stop being confused about something so basic. Let's teach our kids the facts of life and to love life even when that life is only three weeks old in mommy's tummy.

My pastor friend John said, "Mother's bodies are made to be fortresses of protection for developing babies." This is a reminder that every day in America we voluntarily allow, teach, and promote an attack upon the fortress and the vulncrable American baby inside her walled sanctuary; as if the attack is some sort of victory or has virtue. I can't help but connect this image to open borders, allowing our beautiful country and our great people inside her to be harmed. Both are things we had little hope of changing until November 8, 2016.

Think about it.

Oh God, please change our hearts, open our eyes, and help us know real love again. Help us to know too that you forgive us. Help America turn away from abortion and our calloused indifference. May fortresses rise and be symbols of strength and of hope, protecting once again our bright-eyed beautiful future. Amen.

America must once again be the fortress for all created in the image of God, or face the consequences. His grace is sufficient to forgive us both individually and as a nation. That too is a beautiful thing, and as innocent as a baby.

Heartbeats

Congress is holding the "Heartbeat Bill." This law, HR 490, introduced by Iowa's Rep. Steve King, would require a simple test for life. If a heart beats, there is life. As of today, 169 House members are on board as co-sponsors of HR490, officially known as the Heartbeat Protection Act. Call your Congressman to Co-Sponsor this bill. Only the reps with guts and a heroic heart will do it.

Upset and Upsetting

The US budget passed in May 2017 by way of "Continuing Resolution" included funding in the amount of $528 million for Planned Parenthood, an organization founded by eugenicist Margaret Sanger.

Taxpayer funding of PP has doubled over the last ten-year period with 27% more abortions occurring over that same period. PP does 34.9% of all abortions in the United States. PP is a taxpayer supported entity which aborts one child every 97 seconds in America. 887 American lives end every day, paid for with our tax dollars. For years you and I have been forced to pay for this. Source: **Live Action.org**

America has legally aborted at least 54 million American citizens since SCOTUS legalized abortion on demand. Natural born indigenous Americans are missing by the millions and "genius" Ivy League social planners and political scientist attorney types have created an excuse to foist illegal immigration on America as a corrective plan to recover a portion of what we've lost by way of abortion.

The Other Part of the Equation

"If there is a decay of conscience, the pulpit is responsible for it. If the public press lacks moral discernment, the pulpit is responsible for it. If the church is degenerate and worldly, the pulpit is responsible for it. If the world loses its interest in Christianity, the pulpit is responsible for it. If Satan rules in our halls of legislation, the pulpit is responsible for it. If our politics become so corrupt that the very foundations of our government are ready to fall away, the pulpit is responsible for it." *Charles Finney* **Leader of the Second Great Awakening in the United States**

Finney had uncanny insight but surely never imagined the Johnson amendment nor did he envision churches with empty pews as Americans sleep late every Sunday morning, until something happens or someone dies. I hope we are awake, we can't go back to sleep.

The Johnson Amendment: Let the Light Shine Through.

The Johnson Amendment of 1954 is a thick dark veil placed over Christian churches and all nonprofit organizations. This veil must be torn away to allow for strong endorsement or fierce opposition of any and all candidates and for the open debate of all the moral and political or policy issues we face today.

America desperately needs the perspective and reasoning of its civil and spiritual leaders from the pulpits. We have missed their scripturally rich and thoughtful reasoning for far too long. Informed consent or dissent can only occur when Americans are given all the facts available to them. Johnson limited one of the main sources we the people had from which to gather our facts. No one said a thing about it until Trump did. The need to end this IRS-enforced restriction is especially relevant as some news sources refuse to report truth but chose to distract instead. Preachers need to speak and congregants need to listen so that informed decisions can be made once again.

"I believe in Christianity as I believe that the sun has risen: not only because I see it, but because by it I see everything else." – *C S Lewis*

"We the people are the rightful masters of both congress and the courts, not to overthrow the constitution, but to overthrow the men who pervert the constitution" *Abraham Lincoln*

*We are working on it Mr. Lincoln.

Question: If the perverts who pervert the constitution continue in their perversion, does America end up perverted? The choice must be to overthrow and toss those who do.

Chapter 12

The Force

The Dilution

"Government is not reason, it is not eloquence, it is force; like fire, a troublesome servant and a fearful master." *George Washington*

Did you catch the balance and tension in President Washington's description of government? Read it again: *"force; like fire, a troublesome servant* and a *fearful master."* It's a bit like tug of war, with tension on one side from the pull of a servant who should protect and assist us while equal tension comes from the pull of a master who could blaze burning hot to defeat any enemy. One is meant to assist and protect us; the other is meant to defeat our enemies. Both need controlled by us. Both are necessary, both need fuel to stay active, both are force. One may need to be fed in order to serve us, while the other one demands feeding when what it really needs is to be extinguished or at the least diminished.

The servant could, without our directives, become lazy, neglecting its duty, forgetting its role to assist and protect, as with our border and immigration policy, freezing us out, and slowing us down. Think NAFTA or IRS and Tea Party scandal here as well.

The other, without constitutional assertion of our rights and its legitimate role, could consume anything it touches, everything in its path, harming all who lack the strength and determination to choke off its fuel. If directed properly, it will defeat any enemy. Left alone it will spread quickly, taking for itself what it has no right to take and doing what it has no right to do (constitutionally speaking, that is). Think California wild fire fearful master.

Trump is helping to restore the balance in part by draining the swamp. Tension comes when we do our part to control the troublesome servant, requiring it to be America's protector and defender again. Throttling it back, limiting its fuel, and controlling its reach.

Does the fearful master use force more often than the troublesome servant serves? Did our servant morph into our master? A master that basically does what it wants and considers us expendable or simply an annoyance except, of course, during election time? Is it more likely that an uncontrolled master will become a monster, while a servant simply requires instruction and ongoing supervision?

This is one reason the government bureaucracy deep state goons are undermining and resisting the president so fiercely. They grew accustomed to doing most anything they wanted, and loath having restrictions placed on their power. They were led for decades by government sympathizing - I'll scratch your back you scratch mine - administrations. Bureaucracies were created by Congress and Congress keeps funding them regardless of their performance, regardless of their abuse of Americans.

Now, with Trump, they do not seem to want instructional scrutiny or institutional supervision or oversight from someone who's not a career politician and has had a lifetime of managing large entities; building them and keeping them both efficient and subservient to those they serve, that is, in basic business terms known as serving its customer base.

Bureaucrats probably fear their deeds will be exposed as corrupt or just outright wasteful. If so, the fury of the Mighty Middle will require reform and we now have a president who is willing to pull the servant out from the master, out from the monster. Putting the servant back in its proper role while throwing the monster onto the burn pile where it belongs.

Speaking of monsters and burn piles, let's think deep and wide and really big. In the age of Trump, let's do some abolishing. Picture ourselves free of the Departments of Education and Energy. Dismantle those monsters, cut them into fifty pieces and let the states control education again. DOEd has 4,400 employees and cost $79 billion dollars to operate in 2016. We could hire 877,777 people at $90,000 a year each with that amount of dough.

Reagan wanted to abolish DOEd when it was but one year old. Still in diapers and newly fathered by Jimmy Carter his wittle baby consumed "only" $40 billion. Reagan's efforts failed and the baby grew into a monster that won't go out and earn a real living; it demands to be fed by us and threatens our children if we don't. So, we've fed it and fed it and to date this monster has consumed around $2.1 trillion dollars since 1979 with an average of $55 billion every year.

Why are we giving our money to Washington where we have no control over it, only to see it trickle back down to us in the states? The problem is force isn't reason; it's not eloquence and it is a troublesome servant and a fearful master. It was created by a Dem President and a Dem Congress but the Repugs like skipping through its green cascades, too. Let's go long and abolish it. $2.1 trillion. That's a lot of money, folks.

See: downsizinggoverment.org

The Department of Energy in 2016 cost $27 billion dollars. Reagan tried to abolish it too but, "there he goes again", Congress swampiticians ignored him. Today it has 16,000 employees and "oversees" 100,000 contract workers. What does it do for $27 billion? See the **downsizinggovernment.org** site and fill your own think tank.

"All Americans are involved in making energy policy. When individual choices are made with a maximum of personal understanding and a minimum of government restraints, the result is the most appropriate energy policy." --*Reagan administration energy plan, 1981*

Had Congress listened to Ronnie we would have been far better off. Saving this year alone $106 (79+27) billion dollars or to lean conservative cut it in half to $53 billion every year. Again we could hire 588,888 people and pay them $90,000 each per year with that kind of dough.

I think someone's getting ripped off folks, big league.

Remember, George Washington lived under two forms of government; the first controlled by the Crown (King George), the second controlled by the American People.

Both forms contain, by necessity: force. We the people are the force. We are the most powerful branch of government. Go back to the preamble and its 52 words to see the force requirement. Look closer.

Form a more perfect Union

Establish Justice

Insure domestic tranquility

Provide common defense

Promote the general Welfare

Secure the Blessings of Liberty

Force is needed so that we the People can maintain our machine today. Force originates from We the People to our government, which at best is the troublesome servant; the force is then to be projected out from our government into our everyday lives via policy, laws, and procedures. Ideally, government muscle and mind are to promote Unity, Justice, Tranquility, Defense, and General Welfare as it secures the blessings of Liberty for us today and for our Posterity tomorrow. All of us have these things in common and they are essential and worth defending or divided we will fall.

The continuous loop of tension and balance ideally maintains our environment of tranquility and blessings; one where it is self-evident to recognize that all men and women are created equal. An environment where life, liberty, and the pursuit of happiness are never harmed or hindered or We the People rise to make alterations to our government.

The Crown or the fiery fearful English master only cared about the crown. It used force, along with unfair, uncomfortable, unreasonable regulations, to try to keep what it did not own, what it did not develop, what it took no risk to gain, and had no sweat in its creation. It cared little for the individual and certainly did not recognize man's freewill, equality, or man's inalienable rights.

Because of our silence, this is exactly what government has turned into: A Crown of celebrity political nobility, ignoring our concerns, ignoring any comparison to our founding virtues, and ignoring our religious rights, showing favor to only those who fully support it and its growth, making loads of cash while limiting us of the mighty middle. They have used our silence to drain us of our livelihood while filling their swamp with champagne. Today the four richest counties in America surround Washington DC, so what does that tell you? They are entrenched while we are left unstable vulnerable. That is why we must step up and stand with our president.

Our government has become the fearful master, and may still be on the brink of becoming the maniacal monster. So, let's get it throttled back, lower its wick, cut off much of its fuel source, crank down on the big valve, choke its air supply and dial back on that rev limiter.

Our Fuel

Right here, for emphasis, if I were writing a movie script, I'd have a fighter jet scream over us to emphasize the power of this point: *Our consent is Fuel for the Machine.* Swoosh, roar, rumble, afterburner, supersonic, g-force rollover, and out of sight into the wild blue yonder! The jet would be the F-35. One from the fleet that Trump saved us $728 million dollars by renegotiating the price while president-elect. Shows how much his "inexperience" can accomplish.

We the people legally and constitutionally can fuel this machine called government. It should operate and be operated from consent, our consent and our approval, ignited by our vote.

Our vote is so powerful, so dynamic, so earth-shattering, so direction changing. Its power can best be understood as equivalent to the launch code used to arm a nuclear weapon. For its part, the code is rather minor, tiny, and insignificant, and could be contained in the palm or one's wallet, briefcase or in one's mind. Yet once the code is entered, it activates a series of sequential events that unleash a very powerful force capable of mass destruction. That force, accurately targeted, will result in devastating consequences for the intended target.

Well, we did it! We launched the beginning of the bold war. The bold warrior has firmly taken charge and it's up to us to force Congress to comply with our mandates. We want to win again. America First is our mandate.

Our votes are extremely powerful. Don't ever forget it. The enemies of our Republic want us to believe that we don't matter and our vote doesn't matter. Don't buy it. You are, I am, and together we are: the launch code. Powerful together-63 million of us and we are growing, this is despite the press.

Your ideas, my ideas, our concerns, our common sense, our reasoning, our values, and our consent must shape everything government does or doesn't do how it does it, and how much it's going to cost if we are going to secure the blessings of liberty to ourselves today and our posterity tomorrow.

If bad fuel gets into any machine, the result will be bad performance. Try adding a gallon of water to a car's fuel tank. It will run terribly and conk out fairly quickly, I imagine. No, I haven't tested this on my vehicle and you probably shouldn't either. Just think it out. Remember, under Trump, America now thinks again-we must make America think again. As Trump said, "Our Leaders don't have a clue," And it's been going on alongggg time!

MPH vs KL/H?

In the example above, I used the US Customary Measurement System, once simply known as the "Standard" system, using the gallon instead of liter. The Standard system has basically been in use by Americans since the days of the original thirteen colonies. This has relevance today to our Great America agenda; the America First plan and the past "decisions" of our leaders. It's an old subject, but it has application and provides an opportunity to filter out some sedimentary contaminants from our fuel. You may find my laymen's investigation interesting. In fact, the stamp of what I will explain is on your car speedometer and will from now on be a reminder to you.

The "Metric Conversion Act of 1975" was passed by a Democrat Congress with help from Republican President Gerald Ford. The Act ended up being voluntary because Congress had a healthier respect for the people back then and forcing Americans to toss or render useless heirlooms from previous generations like their tools, measuring cups, car speedometers, socket sets, as well as replacing all the speed signs across the country, and gasoline pumps, was just a bit too dangerous for most in Congress, in my view.

So if the vast majority of America was against it, why would our Congress import a foreign system of measurement after we saved Europe and the world from the Nazis? A plan to convert to metric made little sense; were we not the total and complete envy of the world as far as engineering and manufacturing and mechanical aptitude were concerned? We built tens of thousands of planes, missiles, guns, ammo, bombs, trucks, tanks and subs. We were the world's largest market. A market so large the entire world was knocking on our door, begging for the chance to sell their goods to Americans.

Admittedly, Congress did and does today have its own self-preservation instincts, and recognizing an illegitimate child that could haunt them for years, they "allowed" us to voluntarily choose to use the metric system or not. On the surface it seems like a reasonable compromise, one that would take many years to imbed into our industrial systems.

The resulting outcome was that the market slowly, but with high expense and frustrating inconvenience, adapted to metric, yet interestingly, many Americans and businesses refused to convert, which is why today we live with and work with two systems. On an automobile for example, there are bolts, nuts and parts that require metric tools and others that require Standard measurement tools. To me the entire venture was misguided and a waste of resources. What did Americans gain? The mess is still with us today. What does my look back of this issue say to you? Perhaps: watch your Congress closely.

Americans Forced to Conform

What was it that convinced the Democrats and President Ford to change the nation's accepted traditional, successful and distinct system of weights and measurements after more than two centuries of use? This deal occurred long before NAFTA and GATT. This is an obvious example illustrating that politicians have made stupid decisions for us for a long time. Robbing, plundering, and the gutting of America would have continued today had it not been for Trump.

Trump from the campaign trail about our trade deals: **"Our leaders are stupid. Our politicians are stupid. How stupid are these politicians to allow this to happen? We are led by very, very stupid people. We can't let it continue."**

Makes No Cents

Our government continues in a variety of ways to force foreign conformity on us today against our distinctly American traditions. Hop in your car and notice the mph and kl/h. And don't forget these past gems: NAFTA, GATT, TPP, Kyoto, UN, DACA, and UNFCCC. You will find the Progs continually blathering things like "39 countries do this that and the other, so why doesn't the US?"

Here's an example: Climate Change. The Paris Agreement (UNFCCC) where 194 countries signed an agreement to essentially strip American jobs, control American natural resources, and raise our cost of living. The President said no and refused to sign. America today is out and should stay out of this globalist straitjacket. Now we are free to curb our own pollution, which we have been doing very well for decades, and raise our standard of living by providing jobs and restoring industry to produce quality "Made in America" products once again.

If our Departments of Education and Energy were effective with the $3 Trillion or so we gave them over the last 38 years, wouldn't pollution be eliminated and energy plentiful and cheap by now?   Oh, but they would have worked themselves out of a job by now so never mind.

Chiinnaa

China today is a superpower, a communist country with a well-documented history of mass brutality.   American politicians helped China become a superpower by allowing our industries to move to Communist China so we now have to buy Chinese products, including seafood! Isn't America surrounded by oceans?

North Korea is an ally of China.   China has done little to help the US control North Korea's nuclear ambitions or the attack threats coming from them. China could help but it hasn't. Why not? The bigger question is what motivated our politicians to put us in such vulnerable positions to begin with? Stupid!   Wasn't it a Chinese hack of the U.S. Department of Personnel's computer system that compromised the identities of every American government employee and soldier?

What has America gained in trade with China? Very little except having to eventually buy metric tools to supplement our standard tools so we could work on cheaply made foreign produced goods from communist countries using slave labor.

Dilute

The conformist (i.e. let's be like every other country in the world) policies contain a method of dilution. As political scientists and chemists both can tell you, dilution is a very effective tool in the world of chemistry and in the world of ideas. Ideas can become movements and movements involve people. Dilute the people, dilute the idea. Dilute the idea and dilute the strength of the people.

The Progs are constantly trying to dilute our purpose, our ideas, our President, and every single thing he does or is trying to do. Think of it as mass mind control. If we start doubting and lose enthusiasm and go back to Sleepyville, they win. That's why I have added a section at the end of the book specifically for cleaning contaminants from our fuel. Yes, their tactics have worked before but not this time. We are going to win again. We must.

We the people have been diluted or flooded with the concerns of a weak economy, war, terrorism, deficits, drugs, the illegal immigrant invasion, an unresponsive government, high taxes, crime etc. At the same time, we are really busy raising our kids, keeping our marriages strong, working honestly, running our businesses and trying to just have some fun while we do the responsible stuff. They distract us while enacting laws that limit us. One example is when your child turns 17 the additional child tax credit drops off. They aren't an adult until 18 but it drops off the year a child turns 17.

We of the mighty middle do not ask for very much in the way of help from government, nor do we want any help except during serious emergencies. But we are being diluted nonetheless. The intentions of the Progressive Left and their Poli scientists are to continue diluting all that is or was distinctly American. And certainly, without a doubt all that was or is distinctly Christian. The great irony here is that without Christianity, our country and Middle Americans in general would never have been nearly as successful or as triumphant for nearly as long as we have.

I respect the sentiments of **Mr. Joseph Farah**, the founder of **WND.com** (formerly WorldNet Daily). In his must-read book, ***"Taking America Back"***, he wrote the following:

"…the enemies of freedom are the enemies of God," adding **"…it takes a radical agenda to defeat a radical agenda."**

Jesus brought a radical agenda; an agenda that told us to believe in God, that God was his father and God sent him to die for mankind's wicked behavior. To live the agenda out, we simply believe and live by doing to others what we want done to us. Anyone doing us harm is accountable under the basic law, the Ten Commandments. The institutional authority of government then enforces the law upon the lawbreaker. i.e. you kill someone, you die; well, eventually after 35 appeals at 84 years old maybe. You steal; you serve time for your crime and make restitution, etc. Simple. Know that to be part of something great is nothing compared to being part of the kingdom of God. Seek the kingdom first. See the brilliance of it in Matthew 6:33. You will be rewarded - see Hebrews 11:6

Never could I have imagined that our agenda, The Great America agenda, would be viewed as radical, but it is. To retake, reform, and rebuild America; to make America Great Again as one nation under God, in the eyes of some, is a radical concept. I guess we should take that as a compliment from those who can't see what they've done to America or where their policies would lead her. Their policies have definitely harmed her enough already.

"We must always take sides. Neutrality helps the oppressor, never the victim. Silence encourages the tormentor, never the tormented."-- *Elie Wiesel,* Holocaust survivor

Upset and Upsetting

It is upsetting that our past president, Barak Obama, sent $1.7 billion dollars in cash to Iran, definitely without approval from our Congress, along with releasing 21 Iranian spies. Eight months after the payout, Obama finally decided to notify Congress. According to Truth Feed News, May 9, 2017, it is possible, perhaps even probable that $600 million of this cash, *our* cash, went from Iran directly to the terrorist group Hezbollah. Will Congress or the administration do anything about this?

I wrote my Congressman:

Good afternoon Congressman,

I read today an article in Truth Feed News which reported that Obama's $1.7 billion cash payment to Iran has most likely funded the terrorist group Hezbollah to the tune of $600 million. Our tax dollars! Question: Did congress approve the 1.7 billion? Do you believe this should be investigated and perhaps prosecute those involved? Seems serious to me.

In the general election I voted for my representative but he is a bit moderate, taking the side of the Dems sometimes and he is not as conservative as I'd like him to be, nor does he support Trump as enthusiastically as I would like him to. I will wait for his response on the $600 million question and call his office if I don't hear from him. I think his answer will be interesting and reveal something we need to know and we deserve to know, because it is our money. In the near future, if he doesn't support our agenda, the Trump agenda, then I will work for someone who does. I will work in the primary to un-elect him, especially if he doesn't support the wall. Though I do respect him and when I met him found him to be a very respectful, intelligent, friendly, and humble man, he needs to lift the Great Again banner higher to attract more of the independent and Trump Democrats. I would rather him vote like Jim Jordan and Ken Buck and less like Marcy Kaptur or Nancy Pelosi.

Together, we must influence Congress' actions and the laws they are writing or voting on. This is our power. We are the fuel and the more of us that get poured into the tank of the legislature (congress), the more, by our consent, we fuel the machine to make that much needed hard right turn.

Dilution with Danger

Immigration without assimilation is invasion.

Trump: "We will defeat radical Islamic terrorism... but we will not defeat it with closed eyes or silenced voices."

Many of us see some sort of invasion coming. It's obviously happening in France, Germany, England, Sweden and elsewhere, yet our Progressive-led government wanted to open our borders wider to an even greater number of potential non-assimilating immigrants. Some, who the Progs and Repugs claim are fleeing oppression, have intentions to change the America they flee to, into the type of country they fled from. Case in point, Michigan and Minnesota; look at what is going on there.

This looks like a planned and dangerous dilution of American society by inviting in a community who will not assimilate but are sworn to pursue their political agenda of domination by submission. It's not even a hidden agenda either.

I don't recall who said this but it bears repeating, **"I learned everything I needed to know about Islam on 9-11-01"**. After 16 years the march continues with attack after attack around the world and recently eight people were killed on a bike trail by a terrorist in Manhattan. We have learned enough. See: **actforamerica.org.**

Under the guise of religion, we are noticing a long-term political Islamist agenda which intends to fully transfer itself into the free world, using all tactics available; covertly, aggressively and then forcefully. It's a fact, its history, and it can be clearly seen in the rear-view mirror; just look at Europe and Lebanon. This seems like it should be kind of a big deal, no matter which party you're in, wouldn't you think?

Which Tree to Hug?

In the winter, how can we know what type of trees we are seeing while walking through a forest? After all, many non-evergreen trees look pretty much the same; leafless and gray. They're stuck in hibernation, frozen in time; producing nothing at the moment but created to produce some fruit to grow in the season which lies ahead. Spring. Unless we can recognize the type of tree by its trunk, we will only realize what it is in the summer, after it blooms, after it has its leaves, and by the fruit it produces.

Of course, people aren't trees. People can be clever and know that to gain advantage or position will pretend to look like the other men so as to not produce any distinctions that would make them stand out. We must pose an indicative question; do men call out and condemn the terrorism of their fellow man and if not, why not?

Plans of Micey Men

Progressive Dems and Repugs planned to completely ignore facts, logic, and commonsense reasoning by allowing a 500% increase of Middle Easterners to enter America. These arriving immigrants curiously seem to be mostly men of fighting age. They take advantage of the free social services of the host country as they procreate to create a democratic voting majority. It is a well-known fact that they have long-term intentions, even bragging they will build a wave of voters who, with a simple majority of 51%, will control the governments of their host. See Germany see France and other European nations as examples for us. Do we want what they have allowed?

Jefferson's definition of democracy: "A Democracy is nothing more than mob rule, where 51% of the people may take away the rights of the other 49."

"Everybody has a plan until they get punched in the mouth." *Mike Tyson*

The president and our movement is the punch in the mouth to anyone who intends to harm us today or tomorrow.

Empirical Evidence

In 2016, there were 2,475 Muslim-led terror attacks in 61 countries, which resulted in 21,238 deaths and 26,677 wounded. The million dollar question to ponder today:

What is the probable outcome of an open and unlimited immigration policy? What will it do to America and to its future?

Dilute-Weaken and Leave us and our posterity vulnerable.

Yet Progs still want open borders (illegally) and unlimited immigration policy (legally), both diluting America and our culture with their radical policies. The outcome: making us vulnerable while giving them a huge source of leftist leaning new voters. All while running a $20 trillion deficit! NUTS!

The borders were thrown open by Senator Ted Kennedy starting in 1965 with the Immigration and Nationality Act of 1965 and no one has had the will to close them until now, 50 years and millions of legal immigrants later. Why not?

Trump inspired Congress to look closely at the issue. Senator Tom Cotton has introduced the RAISE Act, which is a merit based immigration policy based on the idea that worthy entrants join with us to increase the wealth and strength of our community and not simply come here to glom onto our welfare system. It will end chain migration and the corrupt visa lottery as well. The President will wind down DACA which is nothing more than an end run around congressional authority created by Bo that let 7-900,000 more immigrants in illegally. Current policy allows 1 million immigrants to legally enter America every year. Only 1 out of 15 comes here to work and has a skill. We should pass the RAISE Act quickly. Call Now!

Immigration without Assimilation is Invasion.

Thanks to Trump, we have the opportunity to pause, slow down, and stop everything until we more thoroughly understand the risks. We can then implement measures to reduce those risks. The courts may slow him down, but right is right and we must make America safe again, both for today and for the next generation tomorrow. We will make it safe again by first helping America to think again.

*breitbart.com/big-government/2015/03/30/ted-kennedy

I can't quite figure out how someone can proudly wave the flag of another country but consider it "punishment" to be sent back there. ---*Author unknown*

Why would anyone come to America to change America into the land they left behind?

Ever notice that a small scratch on your car, if left unattended turns into a rusty hole over time? Or that a small chip in the windshield glass grows into a large crack? Preventing a larger problem by reacting to it when it is smaller just makes sense.

Chapter 13

Heavy Meta

"**Laws are made for men of ordinary understanding and should therefore, be construed by the ordinary rules of common sense. Their meaning is not to be sought for in *metaphysical subtleties which may make anything mean everything or nothing at pleasure.**" *--Thomas Jefferson*
*Metaphysical: Abstract speculative reasoning.

Example of Metaphysical: Give money to enemies who have sworn to destroy us. Then allow some of their citizens to enter and live in our country on our social service systems while they have multiple children who are taught to hate us.

Another Example: Purge the schools of any mention of God as creator and purge the Ten Commandments and rewrite history, then ask why our children are behind academically and ending up in prison after spending trillions of dollars on education.

Thomas Jefferson also had great concerns about the SCOTUS and the entire Federal Judiciary and he turned out to be 100% right:

"**...all shall be an irresponsible body...working like gravity by night and by day, gaining a little today and a little tomorrow, and advancing its noiseless step like a thief, over the field of jurisdiction, until all shall be usurped from the states, and the government of all be consolidated into one. (and) shall be drawn to Washington as the center of power.**"

Central power untouchable by the people wasn't the plan; we've been usurped.

The Progs/Repugs own and have fingerprints on their positions. They own a lot of Meta nonsense records.

From their band **"Let America Drift"**

*Meta-Nonsense Records Presents: **Usurping USA***

Along with these other "hits":

Their Russian nonsense,

Their deep state bureaucratic build-up nonsense,

Their over-regulation of Americans nonsense,

Their healthcare takeover nonsense,

Their NAFTA nonsense,

Their illegal alien voter denial nonsense,

Their heroin not stopped at the border nonsense,

Their uranium to Russia nonsense,

Their email server nonsense,

Their missile guidance technology to China nonsense,

Their weak against Islamic terrorist nonsense,

Their weakening our military nonsense,

Their Common Core nonsense,

Their globalism first America pays for it all, nonsense,

Their allowing the God of our forefathers to be thrown out and expelled from school is nonsense,

Their ignoring and censoring of our founders' genius and their beliefs nonsense,

Their bowing down to global warming nonsense,

Their permitting immigrants on welfare for life nonsense,

Their sanctuary cities and now state of CA nonsense,

Their rogue 9th district court rulings nonsense,

Their recognizing international law in US court decisions nonsense,

Their open borders nonsense,

Their toleration of illegal alien crimes nonsense,

Their strengthen government and weaken the people nonsense,

Their complicate the simple with regulations nonsense,

Their help arm North Korea and Iran nonsense,

Their wipe history books of all values and virtues of our past nonsense,

Their ban the Ten Commandments and prayer nonsense,

Their young boys in girls shower rooms nonsense,

Their allowing men who want to be girls go into the girl's room nonsense,

Their Benghazi-caused-by movie nonsense,

Their tax payer funding of Planned Parenthood nonsense,

Their illegal aliens on social services and obtaining drivers licenses nonsense,

Their gag the church nonsense,

Call or write a short note to your Congressman about just one of the issues that really bug you, just one to start.

Establishment Elites

Every "nonsense" position is fact. Whether currently going on or inflicted on us in the past. Nevertheless, they are facts, and they all have negative consequences. When the president or any conservative brings them up, they are shouted down or ignored with a pointed finger questioning their motives.

"One of the greatest advantages of the Totalitarian Elites ... was to turn any statement of fact into a question of motive." --*Hannah Arendt*

And to repeat again George Orwell because the tactic is obvious today: **"So long as they are not permitted to have standards of comparison, they never even become aware..."** The main stream media questions the president's motives and standards:

Fact	What MSM Parrots Say
Border control	*He's racist*
Illegal Immigration control	*He's racist*
Job creation	*He's against the working class*
Extreme vetting	*It's not who we are- just stay dumb*
Control immigration	*He's a racist Islamophobe*
Prolife	*He hates women*

If you think they're going to give us our country back without a fight you are mistaken. Every day is a fight. Proof that even *a*fter one year the left is still spewing toxins into the air. Treating our Great Again movement like we were going to expose their incompetence and negligence and... yes we have!

The retake, reform, rebuild, and restore movement is a strategy to Make America Great Again. By taking our government and country back, away from the hands of the inept, compromising, and self-serving political hacks of the cosmopolitan elite left, we are now able to reform and rebuild American greatness.

It didn't take money to win and begin the take back. HRC spent $1.2 BILLION to Trump's $400 million, so money alone won't do it. It takes votes; it takes us talking to one another about elected officials who are not on board with the agenda the president has been so clear about. He was passionate, clear and concise from the escalator speech on through his taking of the executive branch, and he still is today.

It takes imagination

It takes vision

It takes grit

Devotion

It takes heart

It takes Great Love

"We've been blessed with the opportunity to stand for something-for liberty and freedom and fairness. And these are the things worth fighting for, worth devoting our lives to." -- *President Ronald Reagan*

Liberty freedom fairness-reform rebuild retake, from our 40th president to our 45th, the fight and devotion continue. However it's never just about a president; it's about all of us together. And today it's even more important to be united in all we need to do as Trump leads us forward.

From the Trump rally:

Trump: "I had to do the right thing. I had to do it."

Trump: "We will serve the citizens of the United States of America."

Trump: "We will stop the drugs that are poisoning our youth."

Trump: "I am not representing the globe. I am representing our country. One allegiance: America."

Trump: "I'm just a messenger folks, just a messenger."

Trump: "The silent majority is back and we're going to take back our country."

Trump: "We will put our citizens first. We've for too long traded away our jobs and left our borders wide open so anyone could come in."

Trump: "The era of empty talk is over."

Candidate and now President Trump upset the apple cart by making us acutely aware of the folly of the left. We knew the left was incompetent but no one else puts it under the magnifying glass like Trump. It is distressing to see what the Progs and Repugs have done and allowed to happen to good old America. The good America, not perfect but far closer to the ideal than any other nation; like the one we had when millions of us rode our bikes as kids every day of summer for hours on end, only coming home for lunch and supper.

The good America; where parents didn't fear molesters, drugs, gang murder or human trafficking. Remember that America? Maybe you don't because you have nothing to compare to, maybe you're too young, but it was great, believe me. Our front doors were unlocked and keys left in our cars with trust in each other and in God above.

But God is gracious and He once shed his grace on America; He can do so again. Are we worthy to receive it?

The Judicial Branch

The Judicial branch has far overstepped its authority, violating the separation of powers by assuming power over both the Executive and the Legislative branch. It creates laws and manages or tries to manage segments of our government. Acting like another King George, **"... has refused his assent to laws, the most wholesome and necessary for the public good."** Consider this modest standard from our Declaration, two important connected words "Wholesome *and* necessary".

The Court of Supremes has gutted much of what was wholesome and necessary from our society. We are a hollow shell of who we once were. Parental consent, the Ten Commandments, prayer in schools, and wholesome necessary education have all been replaced by sex education, protected obscene speech, atheism, and open hostility including violence towards most things wholesome. They claim it isn't necessary to teach not to kill, lie or steal, but just to accept everyone and tolerate everything, unless it's conservative i.e. wholesome and necessary.

It doesn't take a researcher with a PhD to see what has happened since we stopped praying for God to bless us, our parents, our teachers, and our country, which once was the outline used for voluntary prayer in our public schools for many decades.

Kids used to pray for their parents, for their teachers and for our nation. In school! An ACLU horror of horrors! No wonder prayer had to be banned. Think about the dangers of that kind of prayer, asking God Almighty to bless parents, teachers and America while in their...*shudder* class rooms!

The opposition says: Such silly stuff, no no no, we will do things on our own because that old-fashioned praying is very uncomfortable for us. Those ten commands, they gotta go because well if a student sees them they might be tempted to obey them. They might then ask where they came from and someone might tell them Moses and if they ask where Moses got them, someone might say God and then that poor kid might actually believe that there is a God and learn that God watches everything they do. They could even end up believing God hears and blesses their prayers, and prepares a place in heaven that's even better than the place he created for them here.

Talk about Metaphysical, this is Meta nutty! Now, in place of prayer and the Ten, we have school killings, rape, teachers molesting students, single parent homes, government corruption, the world's worst academic scores, the highest costs and the list goes on. An over-reaching SCOTUS, a weak Congress who even after JFK was assassinated, left in place the ban of June 25, 1962. The results of the bans go on and on.

Welcome to Lawless City - population minus 2 daily

Chicago 2016 murder rate of 762 deaths

"We have staked the whole future of American civilization not on the power of government, far from it. We have staked the future of all of our political institutions upon the capacity of each and all of us to govern ourselves according to the Ten Commandments of God."--unknown

This quote was once attributed to our 4th President James Madison, the primary author of our Constitution.

Regardless of its original source, the immense benefit of, at our founding and for a century or two, having American citizens and the American government live and conduct business under its canopy, was a source if not thee source of our greatness. The Ten provided protection from criminals, clarity about God, societal order, marital stability, general stability, blessings, warning, justice, self conduct, stewardship, private property rights, and so much more too. The Supremes blew it for America after banning it. But we let them do it.

Jesus taught that the Ten had a summary of Two that would allow us as humans to live together with God's blessing. **"You shall love the Lord your God with all your heart and with all your soul and with all your mind. This is the great and first commandment. And the second is like it: You shall love your neighbor as yourself. On these two commandments depend all the Law and the Prophets."** *Jesus in Matthew 22:37-40.*

See: teachourhistory.com

More evident is what we now live with, because neither the Ten Commandments nor the two great commands are allowed to influence or even be **looked at** by our students. According to the SCOTUS, the Ten Commandments can't even be *looked at* by any student. No student was ever forced to read them, but just in case the unwary student might stop and look at the Ten, stop to read them and even - horrors - reflect upon them and consider any of the Ten applicable or reasonable enough to consider, they had to be banned.

But porn or how to use condoms...that's okay. Meta ridiculous.

Compare Now While We Can

The question now becomes, what did America gain after the court evicted God's ten wholesome and necessary commandments? What took the place of basic, simple, wholesome, yet powerful Godly instruction? What filled the void created by the removal of the foundation for all laws in western civilization?

Again, without a PhD, anyone can see that we now have a society filled with liars, thieves, coveters, illiteracy, mental health problems, suicides, drug abuse, killers, child abandonment, adulterers, STDs, Godlessness, crime, less love, and a whole lot less wholesomeness. And our leaders can't make clear decisions, so we drift towards the edge of...?

Yet today many Prog followers don't agree. They won't see and they don't want to see. They don't want to see the consequences of their decisions and seem to want more of the same types of policies. Crazy but this is who we are up against.

Life is very complicated in America today because the textbook for life from the author of life, law and salvation was deemed to be illegal. What have we staked our future on today? Science, diversity, divisions, money, political parties? How is that working out? Depresso espresso and it isn't very tasty.

"A thorough understanding of the Bible is better than a college education." *Teddy Roosevelt*

A Solution:

Congress, The People's House, must rein the courts in, but how? It's actually fairly simple, and ***Phyllis Schlafly*** revealed how it could be done in her concise work entitled: **"The Supremacists - The tyranny of judges and how to stop it."** Get a copy of the book, you'll learn a lot. Let me quote a little from the author and you will quickly see why Mrs. Schlafly was one of America's all-time greatest leaders and teachers.

"Our task is to expunge the un-American notion of judicial supremacy by using the checks and balances built into our great United States Constitution. We must stop the judicial supremacists who have been systematically dismantling the architecture of our unique, three-branch constitutional republic and replacing it with an Imperial Judiciary. Since the legal community has a vested interest in the status quo, this task *must be undertaken by grassroots Americans. We must raise a mighty demand that Congress do its duty.*"—Phyllis Schlafly

Without a doubt, America owes the late great Mrs. Phyllis Schlafly a great debt for being one of, if not the most consistent Constitutional voice in America, for America, and about American exceptionalism. She had the honor of being labeled "The most dangerous woman in America" by the leftist Progs and "One of the 100 most important women of the 20th century" by Ladies Home Journal.

Thankfully, the president has a good strong list of potential judges who have sworn to uphold our Constitution. Lord willing, his future appointments will free us to be able to once again pursue good and distinctly American ideals for many decades to come, and hopefully we will regain the wholesomeness that once was America. But you and I must help this come about.

An item of interest in The Supremacists is *that several serious consequential court rulings effecting America were done anonymously. None of the Justices would affix their names to their decisions.* Unbelievable.

Let's Get Radical

What if every school board stood up boldly and displayed the Ten Commandments in every one of our schools what would happen? There is something like 150,000 public schools in America. The ACLU can't sue all of them.

Speaking of the ACLU, its founder stated, **"I am for socialism, disarmament, and ultimately for abolishing the state itself as an instrument of violence and compulsion. I seek social ownership of property, the abolition of the propertied class, and sole control by those who produce wealth. Communism is the goal."** ACLU founder *Roger Baldwin*

For more ACLU facts, see the book: *The ACLU vs. America* by Alan Sears and Craig Osten.

Why does the ACLU have hero status in the USA? From what I see, it is simply a huge formidable bunch of lawyers who have intimidated many to back down while Godless socialism is aided and abetted. Apparently there is good money in instability and discord, crime and violence. Job security too?

Progressive Insurance co-founder Peter B. Lewis strengthened the ACLU significantly by donating unprecedented amounts to it as did George Soros of Moveon.org. Look it up for yourself.

Slowly, cleverly, and legally the left has, metaphorically speaking, already burned many of our books and pulled down our historic monuments, like the cross, with little opposition from us or our congress. Statues and plaques put before our eyes tangible reminders of right, wrong, justice, and eternity to name just a few. By banning all things relative to God Almighty, not only have historic God honoring artifacts been removed, they have also removed the reminders about the order God provides and the stability God gives when a nation follows his ways. In their place we now see chaos, distraction and danger; a definite loss of domestic tranquility, yet done so in the name of freedom because someone, somehow, somewhere, was offended and apparently the money was good too.

Look at Venezuela, a country once rich in oil revenues, yet now a raw democracy of mob rule, a dictatorship of corruption. Did they get burned by the promises of Hugo Chavez of the United Socialist Party? Will America do the same someday with Bernie as socialism's mouthpiece and the ACLU as his scalpel, slicing away at wholesome and necessary American ideals? They want to abolish private ownership of property? The question is, what and who's property: land, a house, a farm, a business, a gun, your children, your voice, your vote, our borders? Don't forget, eventually this stuff gets enforced by their whips, their irons, their guillotines, and their firing squads. Think Cuba. Think Again America.

Perhaps it starts first by guys with masks and 2x4s.

Beware the burn of socialism.

Sugar Sugar

If you allow a child to eat whatever they want, and they eat only sugar every day, will they be happy? Yes, for a time. And yes, sugar is a fuel for the body, as are carrots, potatoes, eggs, meats etc. But we know that eating only sugar will hinder the child's physical and mental development. Is a sugar only diet good for him? Will it affect his health or not? Should the parent be held responsible for the child's poor health, and will that parent be responsible to pay for his health care needs in the future. The fact is, the health problems the child will undoubtedly get are directly attributed to the parent, as they allowed this to occur in the first place. The parent was irresponsible for giving in to the demands of the child.

"Oh, but Johnny is happy and getting what he wants. You know, he's really going to throw a tantrum when that sugar is no longer provided." Last question, who ends up losing? Everyone, period.

Lesson: we should stop giving in to the demands of every special interest and do the right things for Middle America again. Especially since we foot the bill, we do the work, and most importantly, it's our right and responsibility to do so.

It's easy to reason that putting bad fuel into our government gives us bad government, right? Bad government pays off big for some, but most of us lose and we have lost big league for the past thirty years.

We lost control of our government, our borders, crime, drugs, property rights, public policy, spending, the courts; you name it we've lost it, complicated it, or watered it down.

Turn it Around

It is interesting to think of the president as a turnaround CEO, a facts and figures leader elected to turn a failing company into a successful one before it becomes too late to recover.

Trump reminds me of Lee Iacocca, CEO of a nearly bankrupt Chrysler in the early 1980s.

Steve Jobs when he returned to Apple, which as of 2016, had 115,000 employees.

Alan Mulally with Ford Motor Company and 201,000 employees. The same Ford that did not take Fed bailout money but chose to find its own way forward out of an economic mess.

Trump has a lot of experience at turning losing ventures into success, as well as creating very successful ventures from scratch. No one like him has ever held office before. Not only is he hard working, he values a dollar; our dollars and he doesn't like waste. A dollar contains effort inside it. It represents our efforts every day as we work. We want our efforts, our work, our sweat, our very lives to be valued and not wasted.

Today, the president has a federal workforce of at least 2.8 million people according to the BLS November 2016. If divided among the fifty states that equates to 56,300 federal workers for each state. Just for comparison, a population of 20,000 is an average sized city, town, village or township in America. There are a total of 22,235,000 people (twenty two millions) employed by local, state and federal governments combined. That amounts to 444,700 government employees (and probably very motivated voters) for each one of our 50 states. You and I are paying their wages. I'm not saying they don't work, or that it's bad or good; it's just that this is a huge number of government ranch hands and until Trump it was a growing number.

All the while, private employment has lost big league. It's almost as if they compensated for a decimated private sector by hiring in the public sector. But who would notice? Could that be called massive wealth redistribution? Building an allegiance with a dependable voting bloc, perhaps?

Consider that in 1989, America had 18,000,000 people working in government and about the same number working in manufacturing. Since 1989, manufacturing employment has dropped to approximately 12,000,000. Manufacturing employment could or should be double what it is today, especially with the size of our population. It is essential for our overall national security to have and to maintain a strong industrial edge; it is in my estimation, as important as having a strong military.

"We have incompetent leadership...we are led by very very stupid people, very very stupid people. We can't let it continue. We lose everywhere...it will change...we are going to turn this country around. We are going to start winning big league." --*Trump*

We of the Great Again 63 are very motivated. It is our right to change our politicians every two years if we need to. It's a right brilliantly built into our constitution for such a time as this. The fact is Trump's agenda is the Middle American agenda. Our Agenda. If our House representatives and senators resist, then they must go. They must be replaced ASAP with someone who will repair the mess they helped create, a mess that *both* parties are responsible for, electing instead someone like-minded who is a Great Again statesman ready to fight the bold war alongside Trump.

Same Game

It occurs to me that we have watched Congress like an audience at a tennis match, as they swat the problems back and forth over the net in the middle of the court of common sense. Our heads move back and forth regularly, volley after volley, showing no sign of a clear winner. After a long predictable game, the audience gets bored, the weather turns bad and substitutes are introduced, yet the same game continues, just with different players. Back and forth.

Status No

The status quo politely volleyed in this fashion until Trump and Middle America purposed that the new status quo would be status NO. NO longer are we going to play this game. NO more loosing. NO more weakness. NO more getting ripped off.

Interruption: news flash - a cold bucket of water moment?

Tiny specs of truth and reality seem to be getting into the minds of establishment Progs and Repugs. There is a growing awareness that, perhaps their positions and their ridiculous false fraud casting about Trump or Russia or ad infinitum hasn't worked and may cost many of them their elections. Some have and will continue to bail or retire rather than face defeat. And defeat them we will. **"Dump da bucket on him Ralphie he's gotta wake up soon or miss da dance party."**

Case in point was Ed Gillespie candidate for Governor of Virginia. Ed campaigned with George W. Bush but ran away from President Trump. Turned out he was the typical all talk no action speak-from-both-sides-of-his-mouth politician. In the middle of the road with a smile painted on his mask he was hit by traffic from both sides. The Motto: Never Trumpers Never Win.

This is proof again that Progs and Repugs are out of touch with reality. They expect us to continue to believe their nonsense and buy in to the old "if it's on the TV and in the newspapers it must be true." Sure it is, Homer, sure it is. Perhaps we bought it in the past because frankly what choices did we have? Trump is now our voice, looking at government with our eyes through the lens of our Constitution and with the wisdom of real-life, real-time experience. He is a father and a grandfather. He works today for their future tomorrow. As do we.

This is such an amazing opportunity; I can't help but repeat it. We the people will fuel the machine so that it takes us where we want to go. We must each use our God-given insight, wisdom, and common sense, perhaps as we've never done before and with new or renewed determination.

Remember, the other side is not going to rest. The big difference is, we will call on the God of our Fathers. He gave unwavering wisdom yesterday; and we need the same wisdom today. We can't rest either, in fact we have only just begun.

President Lincoln at Gettysburg November 19, 1863

On our past:

"Four score and seven years ago our fathers brought forth on this continent, a new nation, conceived in Liberty, and dedicated to the proposition that all men are created equal..."

His vision of our future:

..."that this nation, under God, shall have a new birth of freedom-and that government of the people, by the people, for the people, shall not perish from the earth."

Wise words to reflect on, lean on, and stand on, so we can move out and win again:

Christ: **"I am the way, the truth and the life, no man cometh to the Father but by me."**

Patrick Henry: **"This great nation was founded...on the Gospel of Jesus Christ."**

Abraham Lincoln: **"If we falter and lose our freedoms, it will be because we destroyed ourselves."**

Noah Webster: **"Education is useless without the Bible."**

Dr. Martin Luther King: **"Learn to live together as brothers or perish together as fools."**

I admit I am a cheerleader for Trump. Not so much because of Trump the man and what he had accomplished in the private sector, but because of what he stopped and what he stands for now today.

Dead in their tracks, he stopped the most massive, big government global establishment, political manipulative progressive machine in the history of America from succeeding in their quest to continue their rule over us, and he stymied their plans to recreate America into their image; or as they love to say, "Fundamentally" change America. But change her into what? Do they even know? Because they never explain where we end up if we follow their dreams of Bo's father whispering wind songs only the select few can hear plan.   Things would get better, with hope; nothing very tangible all theory eerie smoke and mirrors. They just needed to do more of what they were doing for another 8 years - sure...easy peasy with a shot of depresso espresso and a piece of delusion illusion on the side.

Best case: Progs are like the dog that chases its own tail so intensely it doesn't notice it is going in circles or the big truck that's about to hit it. But it enjoys itself apparently, believes in what it's doing, and is even amusing to watch for a little while.

Worst case: Tight networks of like-minded radicals cleverly, overtly at work to re-distribute to the world everything we inherited from our forefathers. They move America steadily towards becoming a third world kingdom consisting of only the wealthy and the poor; converting her from a Republic into a raw democracy governed by an elite ruling class trained in only the finest schools on earth.

 Naaaa I'm going with the dog theory. How about you?
"All animals are equal, but some are more equal than others." –*George Orwell 1984*

Chapter 14

Which Will It Be?

"The aim of totalitarian education has never been to instill convictions but to destroy the capacity to form any." *Hannah Arendt*

Destroy the capacity to form any convictions. Capacity defined: *the ability or the power to do, experience, or understand something.*

America… God shed His Grace on Thee?

America…who are you? Who are we?

Just as importantly, who will we be?

What are our convictions today?

Where do our convictions come from?

We must remember first who we were. Past.

Then we will better understand who we are. Present.

Then decide who we will be and how to get there. Future.

On the road to greatness again or will we drift again?

So, we look back to our forefathers. Part of what I have tried to do is look back to them for inspiration. To feel their bravery as they fought a big enemy. To catch their vision as they invented and built their freedom machine. To sense their love as they planned to pass everything on to us.

Everything they did was based on their convictions and vision. And probably their desperation in knowing that if they didn't do what they did then…it would only be more difficult later...more dangerous later...with less probability of success or perhaps no probability of success...

It was their time to rise and to do the impossible.

Are our convictions based on an acute awareness of our current situation? Are they based on the sense that this is our time to rise? Are they based on the idea that no one can do individually what we can do together? Are they convictions that had long been dormant but were ignited by Donald Trump? Are we alive in our convictions? I think the answer is yes, yes we are, and we are more alive than we've been in a long time. We have awakened.

The founders had such strong convictions that they were willing to fight and die for the freedom and rights we enjoy today. Would we be willing to do the same for our country and our children?

Which Will It Be?

Remember the original True Grit movie starring John Wayne? Old, one-eyed Marshall Rufus "Rooster" Cogburn was weathered, weary and often a bit hung over, but always ready to ensure that justice under the law prevailed, especially for a grave injustice like the killing of a girl's father by an ungrateful low life thief.

Rooster often reflected back on a big battle he'd won as a much younger man. In it, he was greatly outnumbered, yet stood up to do the right thing for the right reasons. *Reminded of this great past victory and very determined now to not allow a defeat,* he rode after and tracked down some murderous men. Men who thought they held the advantage; men who knew that most other men would have given up and gone home. In the climactic scene, Rooster speaks to the ringleader of this gang of four evil murderers, Ned Pepper.

Rooster: "I mean to kill you in one minute Ned or see you hanged in Fort Smith at Judge Parker's convenience. Which will it be?"

Ned Pepper: "I call that bold talk for a one-eyed fat man."

Rooster "Fill your hand, you SOB!"

The outcome: One experienced and committed Marshall alive and well and the hero of a grateful daughter who couldn't avenge her father or get legal justice on her own.

But the gang of four overconfident murderous thieves: Dead.

Which Will It Be?

Which will it be for the United States of America? What America will we leave for our kid's kids?

17-25 million Christians who were registered to vote in 2012 did not cast a ballot. As a result, President Barack Obama won re-election by 5 million votes in an electoral landslide. *Source: My Vote Counts.

So essentially, Christians are responsible for not only Obama's victory, but for ALL of his so-called accomplishments, such as: several lifetime liberal Supreme and Appellate Court appointments, same-sex marriage, a 10% growth of the federal bureaucracy, a weakened military, a doubling of the nation's debt, a doubling of heroin deaths, and a foreign policy nightmare involving Russia, North Korea, Iran, China, Libya, the Middle East, and the growth of ISIS.

Where were America's Pastors, Priests, Elders, and Rabbis?

Where were we?

Intentional Efforts and Maintenance

Your home doesn't maintain itself, does it? Of course not, and lying on the hammock doesn't get the roof repaired, the lawn mowed, the carpet vacuumed or the screen replaced. When we stop paying attention and neglect upkeep or prevention, it is almost certain the home ends up having problems that come at inconvenient times. If allowed to go on for too long, the elements get in. The wood rots and the home collapses. There is one near me that is ready to fall down but that very process started a dozen years back. Today, the roof is eye level and all the walls have collapsed. The floor has fallen down into the basement. Wild creatures have moved in and it is a danger to youngsters living nearby. A vivid reminder of entropy and how it affects everything man creates. Even America needs maintenance.

Which Will It Be?

"This election will decide whether we are ruled by the people, or by the politicians." --*Trump*

Politicians have ruled and just about ruined America.

"The choice in this election is a choice between taking our government back from the special interests, or surrendering our last scrap of independence to their total and complete control." --*Trump*

Years back, it was pointed out to me that the first verse of our national anthem, *The Star Spangled Banner*, ends with a big question. Whenever I hear it sung, the question hits and haunts me. It issues a challenge to all of us and to each of us.

"Oh say does that star spangled banner yet wave,

O'er the land of the Free and the Home of the Brave?"

How do we honestly answer this question?

This is not a question for our military only; this is for all and each of us to answer. Does our symbol of unity, purity, bravery, justice, independence, sacrifice, hardiness, valor, vigilance, blood, and heaven wave over Americans that Trust in God and are free?

Francis Scott Key answered the question in the last verse.

Then conquer we must, when our cause it is just,

And this be our motto – "In God is our trust,"

And the star-spangled banner in triumph shall wave

O'er the land of the free and the home of the brave.

What do we trust in today? Are we free? Are we brave?

Can the ideals woven into the flag lift our eyes up beyond our weaknesses and once again help transform us into a free and brave people? You bet, because our cause is (still today) just!

"Those who expect to reap the benefits of Freedom, must, like men, undergo the fatigue of supporting it." --*Thomas Paine* Author of Common Sense 1776

Toss or Keep

We were and I believe still are on the verge of losing and possibly never regaining our individual independence. We can see that many of our representatives are ignoring our Great Again 63 common sense solutions. Our mess took years to get into and will take us years to get out of.

Together, we can toss unresponsive House representatives out of office every two years and senators every six, a beautiful thing.

Remember: 2018-2020-2022-2024 Hike!

We have a chance next and every November and every Spring Primary to issue a verdict on any and all politicians. All it takes is for us to take the time to show up and cast a knowledge-based vote.

I predict that in the early years of President Trump's "turn around America" Presidency, he and his administration will expose the worst of the Progressives from both parties for their corruption and the idiotic policies that have harmed us. (So much has been revealed already after just one year. I can't wait to see what happens in years 2 through 7). One of the goals of this book is to motivate us all to discern who the progressives are and to throw them out of office pronto, before they do us any more harm. Here is how I discern them:

Reminder: If they're not for the wall, toss 'em.

Reminder: If they want amnesty for illegal aliens, toss 'em.

Reminder: If they won't control immigration toss 'em.

Reminder: If they won't require an ID to vote, toss 'em.

Reminder: If they're for sanctuary cities and states, toss 'em.

Reminder: If they won't cut spending, toss 'em.

Reminder: If they didn't help simplify our tax system in 2017, toss 'em and never let the big Gov buffoons ever come back!

"Come November, the American people will have a chance to issue a verdict on the politicians that have sacrificed their security, betrayed their prosperity, and sold out their country." -- *Trump*

Every November, beginning 2018 and in 20 and in 22 and 24.

The offices politicians hold are *our* Congressional offices and if they aren't going to represent Middle America first, and support the president's retake, reform, and rebuild America First agenda, they must be thrown out, booted big league.

It's amazing and so cool that we can choose our leaders and have continuous input through them as to what laws and policies we (ostensibly) want to live under. Ostensibly because its definition is so relevant: "apparently or purportedly, but perhaps not actually."

When we apply this definition to the idea of representation, that we are "apparently or purportedly" through our representatives able to influence law, policy, taxes, foreign affairs, immigration, borders etc, "but perhaps not actually." *Ostensibly* alerts us to a couple things. First: we the people have not been involved; instead we have allowed others to vote and influence our representatives and they obviously poured in the wrong fuel. We've seen the wreck and the carnage in our rear-view mirrors. Secondly, Our Representatives "apparently or purportedly" represent us but aren't listening. Both conditions can be solved if we begin to consistently communicate with them. This includes getting their clear position on issues. We debate with them, we watch them, and at election time we judge them fit or unfit to stand in our place as our representative in Washington.

"Democracy is two wolves and a lamb voting on what to have for lunch. Liberty is a well-armed lamb contesting the vote." --*Benjamin Franklin*

No to Term Limits

I know I said this a page or two ago but it's worth repeating: We the people have all the authority and power we need to toss anyone we want out of the House every two years and out of the Senate every six years. Constitutional term limits work very well when we the people stay informed, involved, and share with others what we have learned. We the people are and must remain the **term**inators and limiters.

Representative government is a machine, and we must be the fuel for the machine. Machines need a continuous fresh fuel supply to function.

Term limits *sound* good, but all they will do is allow most of us to *go back to sleep* under a false sense of security. Congress will end up doing what it does best which is to waste a ton of time chasing its own term limits tail with endless talk and debate thereby allowing other problems to grow into other mountains of mess. Let's not fall into that trap of distraction.

Think this out. Term limits will create unaccountable wild lame ducks that will do what they want in their last term. It also prevents those who are truly good statesmen from having the time needed to "drain the swamp" since all non-elected officials will have to do is wait them out.

Without term limits they are accountable only to us.

If you believe that the last eight, sixteen, or twenty eight years of government didn't work out too well; be reminded again... the machine wasn't the entire problem, it was also the fuel.

Now it is up to us.

I believe we can and must continue to change things. No longer are we helplessly stuck on this jumbo jet while it nosedives towards the ground at terminal velocity. We never were stuck! We just ostensibly thought we were.

House District Fuel -the Great Again 63

There are 435 House Representatives, also known as "Congressmen" for a population of 320 million Americans. We live in congressional districts of 711,000 people. Originally each House Rep was to represent 30,000 people. Yet as America's population increased the number of representatives remained flat at 435, which isn't necessarily a bad thing. This freezing of the number at 435 has served to dilute our influence as individuals but it forces us to organize into blocks or groups in order to get things done. Today it takes 24 of us to have the influence per person that our forefathers had in 1789. One out of 30,000 now takes 24 out of 711,000. That is another reason we need to work together.

I think the folks in the House don't use their title "Representative" as they should. The title alone conveys their job description, and their main duty which is to represent you and me as individuals in the people's house. This can also be seen in the formal title they have, "The Honorable." If they are not doing their job for us in an honorable manner, they are a good candidate for replacement.

The Great Again 63

The House is meant to represent the interests of the people living in house districts. Since all taxes come from individuals, the House has the sole power of the purse. Reps live in the district and can be easily contacted. Federal law, public policy, and regulations will certainly affect all of us. The house is meant for the people of the district to have an individual voice to affect federal law, public policy and regulations. So let's do it.

When 63 of us, or better yet 630, or best yet 6,300 of us living in the district go to the office, go to DC, call the office, or send a note to the office; we will pour in amazing amounts of influence. When this happens, our octane rating goes way up and we will affect the Federal machine. The machine will then be fueled up and available for the President to drive in the direction of Great Again.

You and I can each build a block of at least 63 Great Again voters from our email or Christmas card list - in our district to stay in contact with our house rep and senator to be sure they support our Great Again Agenda. Better yet, if our 63 friends and family each build their own block of 63 we could have 3,969 constituents fueling the machine. What does that sound like to you? BOOM and the Next Stop Is: Great Again Lane.

The Senate

No matter how large or how small, each of the 50 United States has just two senators.

California for example has 39.5 million people and two senators. That's 19,750,000 people per senator.

Wyoming, in stark contrast, has 585,000 people for its two senators. That's only 292,500 people per senator.

Each senator has the exact same power in the US Senate, regardless of their state's respective population. The reason being, they are there to protect the rights of the state and ostensibly of the people and of the governor.

Before the 17th Amendment, senators were elected by their state legislature to keep the 10th amendment and the interest of their state in mind. On average, a senator was elected by 100 legislators from each state. Of course, the link to the people was that each state legislator was elected by the people.

It was a great and brilliant balancing act back then because the House stood with the people and the Senate stood with the States that the people lived in. Tension and balance again. Again… brilliance.

Following passage of the 17th amendment in 1913, senators are now elected by the popular vote of the people of their respective state. This created a problem because it is more difficult to influence or toss a senator who has a six-year term, unless one has massive amounts of leverage or money or they really mess up. The 17th amendment ended up diluting our influence on legislation, but it strengthened our *perceived* voting power. It also removed an important protection for the state. In many states, especially on the coasts, the population is concentrated in just a few cities. Electing senators by popular vote has the Senator more concerned with representing the major cities that elected him rather than the state, resulting in entrenched politicians holding office for decades who are so out of touch with us and us with them that we end up in a mountain of mess, but we knew that already.

Senators like Elizabeth Warren, Sherrod Brown, John McCain or Chuck Schumer can stall, and they have, the president's and our Great Again agenda. We need to toss out these and any senator who doesn't get on board. Many of these guys seem to be more concerned with illegal aliens and keeping our borders open than with the safety and security of Middle Americans. Call, visit, and write them. They may ignore us. It is important we toss em' when their long monotonous six years are up. I think the President will let us know who works with us and who doesn't. We just need to **be ready to roll on race day.**

Senateconservative.com is a great way to find out if a candidate deserves your vote or your boot.

Past Addresses and Future Destinations

Every now and then, I enjoy driving around the old neighborhood where I grew up. I see the house I lived in, the school I learned in, the business I worked at, the homes of people I loved, some that I feared, and many I now fondly miss. Memories, foundations, experiences, and examples; these are all parts of who I am, and who I've become. But afterwards, I always enjoy getting back to our home, our family and our friends. For we are living now, all striving now, all learning now, all hopeful for a better future. It's always so nice to get back home.

Today, my concern as an American parent is: how can we help our family in the future? Are there things we can do now that will help them tomorrow?

The short answers: Stand with Trump. Vote in other Great Again Eagles who stand with Trump. Make the call to build the wall. Pray like it depends on God because it does.

Likewise, a Family Concern

We of the Great Again 63 should look with gratitude in the rear-view mirror occasionally. At the place where we once lived, our 1776 address, the beginning of our journey with principled patriots of great vision and be inspired again by their great examples.

When we began our travels with Trump, we looked left and clearly saw we had veered off the road and became entangled in debris we'd never seen back at our old 1776 address. The windshield was so clouded and obscured we couldn't see very far ahead. To further complicate things, 19 candidates were all telling us how they would steer us out of the mess (that's 17 Repubs and HillBern=19).

In 2016 only one candidate made sense; as he scrubbed off the windshield and pointed ahead to a place much more inviting, a place resembling our former home at 1776. A place God Almighty shed his grace, a place where the people ruled and looked out for each other's best interests.

Today and after Trumps first year in office Americans are already winning again in almost every way possible. Be it jobs, taxes, illegal immigration, defeat of Isis, a stronger military, stronger borders, less regulation, increases in the stock market, housing appreciation, better veteran care, healthcare, opioid eradication and so much more.

Remember that your part in the Great Again 63 helped make all of this happen. The establishment is scared of us. The 2018 elections in November will be brutal, maybe worse than even the 2016 elections. We need to give the President a Great Again Senate to help appoint his Supreme Court choices.

Obama, Clinton, Pelosi and Schumer and others from the far left don't want MAGA to happen and will be fighting us every step of the way. Prepare for battle. Pray that we each do our part.

One side will win, one will not. Which will it be? It's up to you and me.

With our great president at the wheel we have a great opportunity to see America win again for at least the next 7 years. That's good for us today and for our posterity tomorrow.

Lord Willing.

"The Republic was not established by cowards, and cowards will not preserve it." --*Elmer Davis*

Thank you for reading Fuel the Machine.

God bless you as you stand with President Trump to help America win again.

Together we are indeed part of something great.

Most importantly I hope and pray that each of you believes in the name of the Son of God that you may know that you have eternal life.

1 John 5:1 thru 13

See you later or see you in heaven.

**** Please rate this book at wherever it was purchased and spread the word. Thanks ****

To get in touch with me:

Email: info@somethinggreat.net

Tweets to: Self-Evident Truths @ WilliamABooks

Fuel Additives and Boosters

Instructions: Add as needed to keep our think tanks
free of contaminants

**"If we who have freedom don't use our freedom to
preserve our freedom than neither our children nor our
children's children will rise up to call us blessed." --
*Francis Shaffer***

"...then they came for the Jews, and I did not speak out
because I was not a Jew. Then they came for me and there was
no one left to speak for me." --*Martin Niemoller*

**"It's too easy to say "no" to the things that scare us." --
*Tim Foreman***

Are you interested in what our founding fathers believed
and said?   See Bill Federers book: ***"America's God and
Country Encyclopedia"***

Get it at americanminute.com

"If the Nazis had called themselves a religion would we
have allowed them to build compounds across the country?"
Author Unknown

**"It is error alone, which needs the support of government.
Truth can stand by itself." –*Thomas Jefferson***

"Liberty cannot be preserved without a general knowledge
among the people."—John Adams

**"Truth will ultimately prevail where there is pains taken to
bring it to light."—*George Washington***

Discoverthenetworks.org   openthebooks.com

Liveaction.org   downsizinggovernment.org

Theremembranceproject.org   teachourhistory.com

Senateconservatives.com   heritageaction.com

ADFlegal.org   cagw.org

Judicialwatch.org   conservativereview.com

Congress.freedomworks.org   heritage.org

Congress.org   ballotpedia.org

Conservativetreehouse.com   rsbn.tv

WND.com   Understandingthethreat.com

magacoalition.com   ffcoalition.com

PhyllisSchlafly.com   Pewresearch.org

Horowitzfreedomcenter.org   Fairus.org

Leadership institute.org   CRTV.com

Downsizinggovernment.org   Breitbart.com

Hillsdale.edu   Actforamerica.org

Victorhanson.com   Whitehouse.gov

Govtrack.us   Crewexposed.com

Our Great Beginning: Ben Franklin

"I have lived, Sir, a long time, and the longer I live, the more convincing proofs I see of this truth — that God governs in the affairs of men. And if a sparrow cannot fall to the ground without his notice, is it probable that an empire can rise without his aid? We have been assured, Sir, in the sacred writings, that "except the Lord build the House they labour in vain that build it." I firmly believe this; and I also believe that without his concurring aid we shall succeed in this political building no better than the Builders of Babel: We shall be divided by our little partial local interests; our projects will be confounded, and we ourselves shall become a reproach and by-word down to future ages. And what is worse, mankind may hereafter from this unfortunate instance, despair of establishing Governments by Human Wisdom and leave it to chance, war and conquest."

"I therefore beg leave to move, that henceforth prayers imploring the assistance of Heaven, and its blessings on our deliberations, be held in this Assembly every morning before we proceed to business, and that one or more of the Clergy of the City be requested to officiate in that service."- *Benjamin Franklin - Constitutional Convention, summer 1787*

Congressional Math Skills

So, even with our job shortage we continue to invite foreigners in who will work so social security doesn't fail? When the fact is, many immigrants go on welfare for life? Only 1 out of 15 of over 1 million immigrants a year has a marketable skill. That means for every one million immigrants America invites to live among us; only seventy thousand bring a high skill with them. The other 930,000 have low skill or no skill at all. Our welfare costs go up by the billions every year as we run a $20 trillion deficit. It seems to me like Congress doesn't have a calculator for math, nor have they considered what impact this has had on our country. Could you figure this out? Of course! In fact, if you wrote a book on how to wreck a country this kind of stuff would certainly be in it.

That word dilution pops up here again.

We Are

One of my favorite high energy power pumped - hit it hard motivational anthems is called **We Are** by TFK of Canada.

Their lyrics:

But I can't just sit here and watch it!

If we don't stop it no one will.

We are the ones we are the guns and we will ride….. We are the voice of a song unsung

We are the change we are the chains that hold us

We are the choice.

We are the strong.

We are one!

Michigan Rally

Time well spent by Trump was the highly energetic, late hour, last day, grand finale, ringy dingy wow with a capital POW in Grand Rapids, Michigan. Motor City Mountain Man Ted Nugent and his feedback Star Spangled Bannon, oops!

Banner, guitar solo speech, battle cry finger in the eye, American real zeal power rally was a hoot homerun hit. That rally didn't wrap up until 1 a.m. the morning of Nov 8th with Trump arriving as pumped up as his Michigan troops. I watched courtesy of the **Right Side Broadcasting Network.** A Great Again network and destined for great things. **rsbn.tv**

"A wise and frugal Government, which shall restrain men from injuring one another, shall leave them otherwise free to regulate their own pursuits of industry and improvement, and shall not take from the mouth of labor the bread it has earned. This is the sum of good government."--*Thomas Jefferson*

"Never confuse a single defeat with a final defeat."
F. Scott Fitzgerald

"There is no substitute for hard work." --*Thomas Edison*

"Chop your own wood and it will warm you twice."
Henry Ford

"Work hard in silence; let your success be your noise."
Frank Ocean

"I already know what giving up feels like. I want to see what happens when I don't." --*Neila Rey*

"The best books are those that tell you what you already know." --*George Orwell*

"We sleep peaceably in our beds at night only because rough men stand ready to do violence on our behalf."
George Orwell

"There are some ideas so absurd that only an intellectual could believe them." --*George Orwell*

"Make no small plans for they won't stir the souls of men." --*Daniel Burnham* Architect

"Reading furnishes the mind only with material knowledge; it is thinking that makes what we read ours." *John Locke*

breitbart.com/big-government/2015/03/30/ted-kennedys-real-legacy-50-years-of-ruinous-immigration-law/

"Few men think, yet all have opinions." *John Locke*

"For too long, Washington has tried to put us in boxes. They separate us by race by age by income by place of birth and by geography. They spend to much time on what divides us. Now is the time to embrace the one thing that truly unites us. You know what that is: America." --*Donald Trump*

"Americans as a people descended from the same ancestors, speaking the same language, professing the same religion." --*John Jay*

"Being comfortable isn't the way to expand your abilities." *Thomas Perry*

"One does not discover new lands without consenting to lose sight of the shore for a very long time." --*Andre' Gide*

"Raise your words not your voice. Rain causes growth not the thunder." --*Rumi*

"How much should I give? Answer: Give until you're proud." --*Paul Ireland*

"If it is important to you, you will find a way, if not, you will find an excuse." --*Paul Ireland*

"An entire sea of water can't sink a ship unless it gets inside the ship. Similarly, the negativity of the world can't pull you down unless you allow it to get inside you." *Goi Nasu*

"I'd rather stand with God and be judged by the world than to stand by the world and be judged by God." --*Unknown*

"Those who give up essential liberty to obtain temporary safety deserve neither liberty nor safety." *Benjamin Franklin*

"Evil talks a lot about tolerance when it's weak. When evil is strong, real tolerance gets pushed out the door. The simple reason is evil cannot bear the counter witness of truth. It will not co-exist peacefully with goodness, because evil insists on being seen as right and worshipped as being right. Therefore the good must be made to seem hateful and wrong." *Archbishop Charles Chaput*

"The Republic was not established by cowards, and cowards will not preserve it." *Elmer Davis*

"Political problems, at bottom, are religious and moral problems." --*Russell Kirk*

"Our Constitution was made only for a moral and religious people. It is wholly inadequate to the government of any other." --*John Adams*

"God who gave us life gave us liberty. Can the liberties of a nation be secure when we have removed a conviction that these liberties are the gift of God? Indeed I tremble for my country when I reflect that God is just, that his justice cannot sleep forever." --*Thomas Jefferson*

"You can't build a reputation on what you're going to do." --*Henry Ford*

"We in America don't have government by the majority. We have government by the majority who participate." *Thomas Jefferson*

"Every citizen should be a soldier." --*Thomas Jefferson*

"It is not enough that we do our best; sometimes we have to do what is required." --*Winston Churchill*

"The spread of evil is the symptom of a vacuum... there can be no compromise on basic principle." --*Ayn Rand*

Bureaucracy: The most dangerous government entity; given force by congress to, at its own discretion, write its own regs/rules (Legislative powers), enforce its own rules (Administrative powers), and judges whenever it deems its rules are broken (Judicial powers). Having all three powers is dictatorial and a danger to every citizen and their property. This was the very danger we threw off when we booted England's King from our shores and wisely separated those powers in our constitution. Why then and not now?

Out of a life of luxury he steps into the world of politics with little to gain. He had heard the distress of the people. He takes all the risks. He learns as he goes. He assembles a team to win and to rebuild again. He builds a wall. His name: Nehemiah.

"If not us, who? If not now, when?"--President Reagan

For years I wanted to write this book but there was always something missing. It took Donald J. Trump to fill in all the blank pages. I hope you enjoyed it, better yet I hope you stand with us. There are many good things to see on the road ahead. —William Andrew